POWER PLAYS OF THE WEALTHY

*How to Retire Early,
Supercharge Your Cash Flow,
and Minimize Taxes*

POWER PLAYS OF THE WEALTHY

How to Retire Early, Supercharge Your Cash Flow, and Minimize Taxes

MARC HENN

ethos
collective

Printed in the United States of America

Published by Igniting Souls
PO Box 43, Powell, OH 43065
IgnitingSouls.com

LCCN: 2024921293

Paperback ISBN: 978-1-63680-407-1
Hardback ISBN: 978-1-63680-408-8
eBook ISBN: 978-1-63680-409-5

Available in paperback, hardcover, e-book, and audiobook.

Any Internet addresses (websites, blogs, etc.) and telephone numbers printed in this book are offered as a resource. They are not intended in any way to be or imply an endorsement by Igniting Souls, nor does Igniting Souls vouch for the content of these sites and numbers for the life of this book.

Some names and identifying details may have been changed to protect the privacy of individuals.

The superscript symbol IP listed throughout this book is known as the unique certification mark created and owned by Instant IP™. Its use signifies that the corresponding expression (words, phrases, chart, graph, etc.) has been protected by Instant IP™ via smart contract. Instant IP™ is designed with the patented smart contract solution (US Patent: 11,928,748), which creates an immutable time-stamped first layer and fast layer identifying the moment in time an idea is filed on the blockchain. This solution can be used in defending intellectual property protection. Infringing upon the respective intellectual property, i.e., IP, is subject to and punishable in a court of law.

To my wife and best friend Ruth.
Without you, life would be so.....ordinary.

TABLE OF CONTENTS

WHAT IS A POWER PLAY? 13

PART ONE: PENALTY

CHAPTER 1: PRODUCERS VS. CONSUMERS 19
    Leveraging Like the Wealthy. 20
    Transformational Wealth 21
    Leverage the Incentives 23

CHAPTER 2: UNDERSTANDING TAXES 27
    The Rest of the Story. 28
    You Control How Much Tax You Pay. 30

PART TWO: POWER PLAYS

CHAPTER 3: INTRODUCING THE PLAYERS 35
    Five Super Asset Classes 36
    The Fine Print. 38

CHAPTER 4: BUILD A BUSINESS...................41

What Kind of Business Should I Start?......41

Leverage Other People's Money...........45

Leverage Other People's Time............46

Leveraging Technology 46

Power Plays 47

CHAPTER 5: THE WORLD OF REAL ESTATE.................51

Types of Real Estate 52

The Magic of Depreciation 53

More Benefits When You Sell
Your Real Estate 56

Extra Real Estate Opportunities 60

Power Plays 61

CHAPTER 6: CAPITALIZING ON OIL AND NATURAL GAS.........63

We Need Energy......................64

Oil and Gas Ownership.................65

Other Oil and Gas Opportunities 68

Limited Partnerships 68

Oil and Gas Mineral Rights 68

Oil and Gas in Retirement Accounts.....68

Oil and Gas Opportunity Zones.......69

Power Plays 71

CHAPTER 7: PAPER ASSETS 73

Stock and Bonds 74

Paper Assets as a Business 75

For the General Investor 78

Private Equity 82

Power of Compounding.................84

Power Plays 87

CHAPTER 8: OTHER COMMODITIES.....................93

The History of the Dollar 94

Cryptocurrency 95

CHAPTER 9: SUPERCHARGE YOUR POWER PLAYS............ 97
   Super Power Plays 98
   The Ultimate Power Plays 103

PART THREE: PREVAIL

CHAPTER 10: MAXIMIZE YOUR POTENTIAL 111
   It's Time to Put the Power Plays
   to Work for You......................113

APPENDIX: QUESTIONS TO ASK A RETIREMENT PLAN PROVIDER ...115
ENDNOTES................................117
ACKNOWLEDGMENTS..........................119
ABOUT THE AUTHOR 121

FOREWORD

I love everything about this book: the author, the title, and the subtitle. Who doesn't want to master: *The Power Plays of the Wealthy*. And last time I checked, these three benefits are incredibly valuable: *How to Retire Early, Supercharge Your Cash Flow, and Minimize Taxes*

Marc doesn't shy away from the truth, offering a candid look into the mindset and methods of the super successful, the first book in the Transformational Wealth series.

Marc has taken the complex investing world of high-net-worth individuals and distilled it into actionable strategies anyone can understand and implement. His Power Plays inject confidence about the upper limits of what's possible.

He has created detailed financial strategies for each of the five asset classes to minimize taxes and super-charge your cash flow, and then he shows you how to combine Power Plays into Super Power Plays until you are investing effortlessly across multiple asset classes.

Thanks to decades of experience, Marc found a way to make it simple and easy.

As an entrepreneur and author myself, I recognize the power of turning knowledge into multiple streams of income. Marc's insights in this book have the potential to do just that for you. He serves as your guide and sherpa through the treacherous terrain of financial success.

In a world where most people leave their financial future to chance, *The Power Plays of the Wealthy* empowers you to take control. It gives you the financial toolkit you need to create value, build legacy, and achieve the kind of freedom you need to make a real impact in the world.

—Dr. Kary Oberbrunner, CEO of Igniting Souls,
Wall Street Journal and *USA Today*
bestselling Author of 14 books

WHAT IS A POWER PLAY?

Power plays give hockey, lacrosse, cricket, and roller derby an added boost of excitement. These contact sports put players in a sort of time out when they break the rules. Then, when one team is down a player, the other team has two or three minutes of superiority. It's time to move into action and take advantage of the opportunity provided by the rules of the game. Fans feel a bit of aggravation when their teams don't score during those few minutes of dominance.

I feel that same frustration when I see people missing out on the Power Plays in the financial world. Many think the dispersion of assets and wages in our country isn't fair. When you look at these charts that show how much of the wealth and wages falls within the top 1 percent of the population, you might be tempted to agree.

Average Wages of Top Earners	
Group	**Average Wages**
Top 0.1% of Earners	$3,312,693
Top 1% of Earners	$819,324
Top 5% of Earners	$335,891
Top 10% of Earners	$167,639

Source: Economic Policy Institute, based on 2021 Social Security data

Wealth Category	Total cohort wealth (share)	Wealth per household
Avg wealth across all households	$143.72 trillion (100 %)	$1.09 million
Avg wealth - top 0.1 percent	$20.05 trillion (14.0 %)	$1,525,480,469
Avg wealth - 99th – 99.9th percentile	$23.9 trillion (16.6 %)	$18,367,709
Avg wealth - 90th – 99th percentile	$52 trillion (36.2 %)	$4,395,954
Avg wealth - 50th – 90th percentile	$44.09 trillion (30.7 %)	$838,634
Avg wealth - bottom 50 percent	$3.68 trillion (2.6 %)	$55,998

Note: Figures do not add up to 100 percent due to rounding.

Sources: Households data from FRED; wealth data from the Federal Reserve, with figures as of Q2 2023

However, how do you think the top 1 percent of wage earners and asset holders get into that spot and stay there? First, it takes work. But on top of that, they use strategies—Power Plays—to maximize every advantage.

For thirty-five years, I've been studying investment and tax strategies to find the best structures to use for gain—techniques I did not learn while getting a degree in economics or studying to become a CERTIFIED FINANCIAL PLANNER® professional. And because it seems like no one really teaches these approaches to wealth, many qualified planners and tax advisors, who may file superb tax returns, can't have a discussion about the financial Power Plays high-wealth clients use. That also means they don't understand how to put these tactics to work for the average investor.

I have a client who brings in a significant yearly wage. It took some doing, but I finally convinced him to invest in oil and gas. Waiting on the annual tax reports for these investments can be exasperating. The tax statements usually come right before the filing deadline. So, the client felt frustrated. When the documents finally arrived and he saw the tax savings this investment gave him, he said, "Marc, I don't care how late this paperwork comes if that's the kind of tax advantage I can get!"

That's why I am writing this book. I want everyone to experience the freedom implementing these strategies can create. Thomas Jefferson often used Sir Francis Bacon's phrase, "Knowledge is power." I want to give you power.

You can experience financial power if you understand the five

I want everyone to experience the freedom implementing these strategies can create.

super asset classes[IP], the tax savings they can create, and the risks they present. Yes, these powerful investment strategies have some risk attached to them, like all investments, but with an advisor who understands them guiding you, you can minimize risk, maximize tax savings, and enjoy your money instead of sending it to the IRS.

But tax reductions are just the beginning. Each asset class has some unique Power Plays—ways to take advantage of the rules and score big—just like in hockey. I feel energized when I start telling people about these opportunities that have the potential to supercharge cash flows in addition to the tax savings. I love seeing the look in people's eyes as we start to explore ways to help them reduce taxes, grow their wealth, and potentially retire early if they choose.

In the next pages, I'll reveal the mysteries and investing strategies of the five super asset classes. If you've already begun to build wealth, incorporating these can provide the investment landscape to produce financial gain, increase cash flow, and bring significant tax reduction.

But what if you're still working a nine-to-five? Maybe you thought the ultra-wealthy had exclusive rights to the tricks of the trade. If you're just taking your first steps into the realm of Power Plays, I've got exciting news. Those willing to commit to the strategies you uncover here may well find more freedom, flexibility, and the opportunity to escape the everyday rat race.

Every bookstore has at least one shelf of wonderful financial books on how to avoid this nine-to-five life, invest in real estate, take the fast lane, start a business, and more. Few, if any, show you how to create an investment and tax minimization game plan. But shouldn't everyone be able to benefit from financial planning like the wealthy and invest across multiple super asset classes? I can't wait until you begin to see how you can use these strategies to invest, pay less in taxes, and experience more financial freedom like the wealthy. It's time you leveraged these layered tax savings to build wealth for yourself—strategies I call the Power Plays of the Wealthy.

PART ONE
PENALTY

CHAPTER ONE

PRODUCERS VS. CONSUMERS

The United States Tax Code's nearly 7,000 pages seems intimidating. Add the IRS guidelines and regulations and you'll find a daunting 75,000 pages.[1] However, most people don't realize that only a portion of the document tells you how to pay your taxes or how much you owe. The bulk of the instructions explain how to minimize, reduce, or get rid of taxes. But if you don't understand the basic principles and tactics the wealthy use, the tables are stacked against you before you begin.

The average person wonders how the wealthiest people in the land—the Michael Bloombergs, Jeff Bezos, and Warren Buffets of the country—reduce their tax burden to an effective rate that is very low or even nonexistent. Some don't think it's fair. Others believe these high rollers are hiding money, using secret loopholes, or cheating the system. But what if I told you they're simply using the tax code to their advantage?

They pay experienced tax and wealth advisors to employ every legal strategy to reduce the amount they owe, and these same benefits are available to every person who pays taxes.

Leveraging Like the Wealthy

Leverage is a powerful tool. Sailboats leverage the wind to gain speed and travel across the seas. Pulley systems use leverage to reduce work by changing the direction of force. Each rope and wheel we add to the mechanism reduces the amount of energy needed to move the load. In every case, leverage allows you to gain more with less effort.

I learned to implement leverage relatively early in my entrepreneurial journey. Cutting neighborhood lawns has been a tremendous first business for teens for decades. But there are only so many hours of sunlight each day. So, as my business grew, I leveraged the power of a riding mower to increase the number of lawns I could get through each day, doubling and tripling my bottom line. When the business grew even more, I leveraged the time of other teens I could trust to mow for me. My equipment, my fuel, and their time meant I made money without even being at that neighbor's home.

Tax laws provide built-in opportunities for leverage. In nearly every asset class, individuals who build wealth leverage those rules with OPM (Other People's Money), OPT (Other People's Time), and technology to reach financial freedom.

OPM can help you start a business—something Robert Kiyosaki, author of *Rich Dad, Poor Dad*, recommends everyone do to maximize the tax benefits. I know many people feel safer working for someone else. But if you have an idea and a bit of entrepreneurial spirit, you're probably like me. I think owning my business is safer. I have control. No one can fire me or lay me off.

Many people start their businesses as side-gigs. They leverage OPM through loans and some use credit cards. Then, as their businesses grow, like I did with my mowing enterprise, they can start leveraging OPT. Even before you quit your nine-to-five, you might bring on staff to help build your company.

One of the greatest things we can leverage is knowledge. Every bit of information has the potential to take us closer to our goals if we use it to our advantage. That's why understanding the five super asset classes and the Power Plays they offer is vital to joining the wealthy in this game of money management.

> **One of the greatest things we can leverage is knowledge.**

You've probably been leveraging time, money, assets, and more all your life without even realizing it. I want to show you how to put this advantage to work for you with purpose. When we leverage with intention, we can see our money grow and bring others along with us. This book is not about growing wealthy while everybody else gets poor; I believe this process can benefit everyone. I want to help you, and I want you to help others.

Transformational Wealth

I grew up in a comfortable home with two working parents who eventually divorced while my brother and I were in school. They were both supportive where they could be, but their jobs stopped them from being involved as much as they would have liked during sports seasons, and that created some problems. You see, in high school, my older brother ran track, and I played football. During my senior year, they came to every one of my home games. Is there anything better than Friday nights under the lights? But track meets were a different story.

Dad and Mom both taught school about twenty miles from our home in a different district than the one my brother and I attended. Because track meets were held right after school, by the time our parents finished their day, did the prep teachers do after school, then drove back into town or tried to get to an away location, the meets were over. Do you think one of us felt less important?

Everyone looks at wealth from a different perspective. In my family, even my parents felt my brother got short-changed his senior year because they couldn't make it to many of his track meets. When we begin to have this wealth conversation, we need to consider relationships, experiences, health, education, wisdom, support systems, and more.

I believe financial net worth falls into the lowest form of wealth categories. Those funds you have invested or accumulated in your savings account aren't worth much if they don't support all the other areas of wealth. If your net worth is in the millions, but your children never see you, are you truly wealthy? If you have a Fortune 500 business, but your health deteriorates to the point you can't go to the office after you turn forty-five, have you really succeeded?

Granted, you might not be able to be there for every important moment, but transformational monetary wealth undergirds the most abundant lives. It allows you to make memories, take care of your physical and spiritual health, and create experiences you otherwise might not have. That's why I have a passion to help people leverage the Power Plays of the super asset classes. I don't want to simply help people make more money; I want the tips you'll find in this book to free you to spend more time with your family, plan get-aways with your siblings, and enrich your life with travel, hobbies, or an investment of time into your community. The list is endless.

Leverage the Incentives

Understanding the basics of the five super asset classes can change the trajectory of your financial life. However, first we have to answer the question, "Why does the IRS offer so many incentives and tax cuts to the richest people in the country?"

The simple answer—they don't.

Every incentive and tax cut the wealthy leverage is available to you and me. We have to choose whether we want to take advantage of the strategies or fund those who do. Millions of Americans unwittingly participate in the incentives by providing tax dollars for others to use to build their wealth.

> Every incentive and tax cut the wealthy leverage is available to you and me.

People's actions put them into one of two categories—producers or consumers. Producers are those who use their money to build the economy. They invest in other businesses, build apartments and homes, create jobs, and provide places and opportunities for people to get the things they need, and better their lives through education and the arts. Consumers use those homes and jobs; they shop in the businesses and enjoy the entertainment.

There's absolutely nothing wrong with being a consumer; however, consumers who aren't also producers don't get tax breaks. On the other hand, if you're willing to use your money to make the lives of those around you better, the government provides incentives. The wealthy focus on production. Ideally, they realize when they help society, they help themselves.

Let's face it, the government needs a happy, content population, so they create benefits for people who feed this goal. Without jobs and places to buy groceries and live, people would quickly grow discontent. That's how anarchy starts.

Yes, some wealthy individuals use government incentives with no altruistic motives. They build their lives as producers until they can escape from The Rat Race. But we hear even more stories of people like Danny Thomas who used his wealth and influence to build St. Jude Children's Research Hospital. While I don't know which tax incentives Mr. Thomas might have taken advantage of, I know leveraging tax strategies probably gave him more money to use to help others. Plus, his producer mentality and his heart to help the hopeless impacts more than eight thousand children every year[2], and his legacy will live long past his children and grandchildren.

What would you do if you could escape? Buy a chalet in the Swiss Alps? Purchase a 400-unit storage facility? Build an orphanage in an underprivileged community or developing country?

Chapter 1

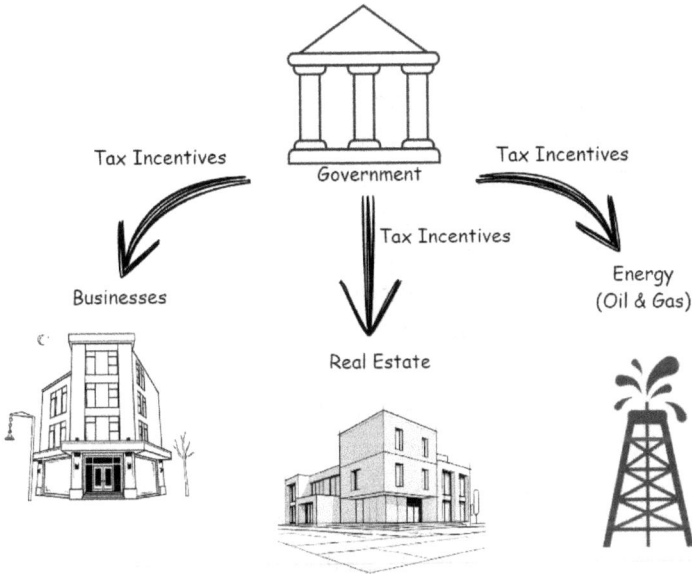

The best producers look for what their community needs and fill the void. They've built factories, stores, housing, libraries, hospitals, and churches. The list is endless. Unfortunately, while every producer becomes a consumer when he or she needs something, not every consumer is a producer. How do you know which category you fall in? Well, let me share a couple signs in comedian Jeff Foxworthy style.

- If you can't find money to put in a 401(k), but buy six-dollar lattes every day, you might be a consumer first.
- If you can't find time to start a business, but never miss a football game on television, you might be a consumer first.

- If you "need" the newest model smart phone when it comes out, you might be a consumer first.

By shifting your focus to producer, you can take advantage of the tax strategies that allow the wealthiest to reduce or eliminate their tax burden. You might not be able to put every tactic into place in your financial life right away, and focusing on too many at one time has the potential to split your attention. Some of these strategies have special rules, and others require a bit more effort and research. I recommend focusing on the one that intrigues you the most and after you've mastered that, add another.

To achieve the greatest success, consult a fee-only advisor. Someone with knowledge in these tax and investment strategies as well as being willing to work with your accountant. You might have an excellent CPA; however, there's a good chance they don't know all the laws attached to these super asset classes. It's not their fault, they don't have to deal with them on a daily basis.

So, let's get started by looking at some of these laws and how you can harness their power to become wealthy in every area of your life—relationships, health, wisdom, and finances too!

CHAPTER TWO

UNDERSTANDING TAXES

Taxes have been around at least as long as Rome, and even in Bible times, the tax collectors were not popular men. The Boston Tea Party received a prominent place in history when it became a catalyst for the Revolutionary War because the colonists didn't like high taxes on their beverages.

In her infancy, the US had only a few tariffs/excise taxes—much like sales tax—on goods like alcohol and tobacco. The states collected the money and passed it on to the Federal government. Even amateur history sleuths have run across government records of taxes on cattle, horses, and other personal property, but this didn't last long.

In 1861, to help with the war effort, the government imposed the first income tax. When the Civil War ended, the Supreme Court declared the tax unconstitutional. Afterwards, those in office attempted to put an income tax system in place, but each time the courts shot them down. Finally, in 1913, under the guise of a Robin Hood-style tax that took money from the rich and gave it to the poor, the Sixteenth Amendment was ratified, allowing the government to levy an income tax.

It was a rough time in America. The industrial revolution brought with it long hours and unsafe conditions courtesy of the Carnegies, Rockefellers, and Morgans. History calls them robber barons. Unions began to rise in power and factory workers started to understand how little these moguls could accomplish without them. So, the average American didn't feel a bit bad about taxing the powerhouses they felt were stealing their lives.

The Rest of the Story

As the Office of the Commissioner of Internal Revenue moved from excise taxes—which had grown to include every commodity possible, including tea—to income tax, they increased the number of tax categories. Separate tax categories for capital gains and write-offs for depreciation and other business expenses started hitting the books. The poorest in the country didn't need the deductions, and those in the middle class either weren't eligible or didn't know about them. And this is where the rubber meets the road: While the idea of the ultra-rich carrying the bulk of the load in building America's infrastructure and government sounded good, in reality, the burden of taxes fell to the middle class. Unfortunately, it's a situation that still exists today, and the middle class in this country doesn't even realize it. I can't do anything with the eligibility. However, I have a goal to do what I can to end the lack of knowledge. You shouldn't pay taxes simply because you don't know the laws.

When politicians brag about raising taxes on those with the highest ordinary income—the level most of those politicians live in as well—they don't tell you that the wealthiest strategically avoid the higher tax brackets. The special tax laws for capital gains, depreciation, intangible drilling costs, and business expenses rule them out. It won't matter how high they raise the tax rate for the highest ordinary income tax bracket, only those who don't use the tax laws to their advantage will be affected.

Most people aren't aware of the fact our country employs three different tax systems, and the wealthy use the best parts of each to minimize their tax burden. Before you can use the asset classes to minimize your tax, you need to know which tax class your finances fall into.

1. **Tax on what you earn**—Everyone is familiar with income tax. Individuals, small businesses, and corporations all pay this tax. This category also includes Social Security and Medicare taxes (FICA), taxes on retirement income, and taxes on dividends and realized capital gains.

2. **Tax on what you buy**—We each pay sales tax every day. However, this also includes value-added taxes, tax on gross receipts, and excise taxes.

3. **Tax on what you own**—States, parishes, counties, and the federal government impose a variety of taxes on property, estates, inheritances, and wealth.

You Control How Much Tax You Pay

Most of us are too familiar with income tax. Individuals see it right on their paystub. And for both the W2 employee and the self-employed, if you're making six figures, a portion of your income may end up being taxed at the highest income tax rates. Not only do you pay income tax on your gross income, you also pay employment taxes such as FICA (Federal Insurance Contributions Act). W2 employees pay over 7 percent into these retirement taxes, and the self-employed pay double.

The regular tax on earnings also includes everything the government calls ordinary income—money you receive monthly from your retirement plans, 401(k)s, and IRAs. While you avoid employment taxes on these funds, they can push you into a higher tax bracket, especially if a large portion comes from income that is tax-deferred.

Everyone understands earned income; however, few are familiar with converting earned income (salary and wages) and ordinary income (without tax benefits) to create passive (e.g., real estate, oil and gas) and portfolio income (e.g., qualified dividends and long-term capital gains). This is how the wealthy position their assets.

Everything we make on businesses, real estate, oil and gas, and paper assets, including long-term capital gains and qualified dividends, receives special treatment. Rather than being taxed at the highest rates of ordinary income, which is currently 37 percent, these special asset classes currently offer significant tax savings through the use of depreciation, tax credits, amortization and for being on a different tax schedule, for example, capital gains. Additionally, some tax environments, for example,

Roth IRAs and Roth retirement plans, allow for special tax treatment.

Taxes are the biggest expense every working person and investor faces. They steal more than money from you. They take your time because you have to work additional hours to make up the difference. And that time robs you of building other wealth, like relationships. However, for

> Taxes are the biggest expense every working person and investor faces.

those willing to contribute to society—become producers—there are advantages. Shifting your mindset from consumer to producer provides enormous benefits. And understanding the strategies I share in the following pages, especially the way the tax system works in favor of the producer, can hugely impact your financial future.

The government doesn't mind taking our money. If we aren't willing to roll up our sleeves and do the work, they will tax us to the fullest. Though the tax code offers plenty of benefits for even the smallest investors and entrepreneurs, the IRS has no intention of helping you figure out how to use them. If we aren't willing to fight for ourselves, we can't take charge of our financial freedom.

Every working person will eventually invest in the economy. Consumers, who tend to be a large portion of the middle class, "invest" through taxes. Producers—investors and business owners—get to choose where to enhance society. Plus, for their trouble, they receive tax benefits and increased wealth.

The amount you pay in taxes is entirely up to you. If you're willing to be a producer, work to structure your assets in the most profitable way, and convert your income to passive and portfolio income, you can use the bulk of the tax code to your benefit. By leveraging the Power Plays of the Wealthy, you have the potential to increase your time, health, relationships, and assets. It will take some work, but with a little knowledge and determination on your side, anyone can play the game.

PART TWO

POWER PLAYS

CHAPTER THREE
INTRODUCING THE PLAYERS

Before we go any further, it's time for me to introduce you to the key players in our story. While you've probably heard of all five, most people think they only live in the pocket of the wealthy. The average middle-class individual might dabble in one or two, but few understand the huge advantage wielded when we move two or more into action in tandem.

Imagine your financial life as a hockey game. Your opponent is the government tax system, and your paycheck is the goalie. If you aren't putting any of the super asset classes to work for you, it's as if everyone on your team except your goalie is in the penalty box. Your paycheck tries to keep the other team at bay, but they just keep scoring.

Each asset class could be a player on your team, and with every one you add, you move into position to start to dominate the playing field. In fact, these players are so strong that every time you put one in, it feels like your opponent lost a player. Soon you're scoring with almost every shot because you are taking advantage of the Power Plays.

Five Super Asset Classes

I'm going to dive deeper into each of our five players, but first, let me give you a brief introduction to the asset classes.

Chapter 2

5 Super Asset Classes

Businesses

Paper Assets

Real Estate

Other Commodities
(Gold/Silver)

Energy
(Oil & Gas)

1. **Business**—Every election, we hear how the current administration has handled the employment rate. For some reason, we expect politicians to make sure everyone has an opportunity for work.

And let's face it, those who don't work, don't pay taxes. It's in the government's best interest to have everyone working. That's why businesses get tax incentives and it pays for you to think about starting one of your own.

2. **Real Estate and Housing**—This is more than just buying your own home. People need places to live and do business, and the public gets upset when affordable housing isn't available. For the most part, the government also doesn't want the headaches of being a landlord, so they give more incentives to those who make space available in the private sector.

3. **Energy**—As a nation, we enjoy being warm in the cold months and cool when it's hot. We like being able to fill up at a gas station or charge our EVs easily. When energy prices go up, voters start to blame Congress or the president. The government needs the private sector to lead the charge in boosting energy supplies and funding research, so they incentivize most energy investments.

4. **Paper Assets**—Most of us are familiar with stocks, bonds, options, futures, mutual funds, IRAs, 401(k)s, and more. When you invest in paper assets, you're investing in businesses–either new or existing. With private investments, you're helping an entrepreneur or business by providing a capital infusion to add people, technology, marketing, and so on for future growth. When purchasing investments in the public sector, for example, an equity on the stock market, you are buying ownership in a corporation and you get

to participate in the successes and failures of that company.

5. **Other Commodities**—While gold, silver, precious metals, and other commodities offer little in the way of tax advantages (we will throw cryptocurrency into this category for now), they do provide innovative ways to protect the wealth that has been created.

Many use these five super players to help move ordinary and earned income into passive and portfolio income, bringing tax savings as well as more cash flow. But knowing what they are isn't enough. Knowledge without action is like recruiting players but not putting them in the game. Now that you have these five players on your bench, how will you put them in the game?

> Knowledge without action is like recruiting players but not putting them in the game.

The Fine Print

Though these asset classes have tax incentives and often provide greater wealth opportunities, they also carry risk. If you've ever dabbled in the stock market, you already know the stocks that promise the highest returns typically come with the greatest volatility. Investment equals risk. Putting your money in a bank minimizes the danger, but that's why your savings and checking accounts pay little to no interest every year. The only risk-free financial opportunity might be putting gold in a fireproof box bolted to the floorboards under your bed.

But your bedroom doesn't pay even miniscule interest, and the price of gold may fluctuate as well.

I could write an entire book on each one of these super asset classes. My goal is to give you an introduction to these areas so you can begin your journey. Additionally, each asset class has a variety of tax structures—more than I can possibly cover completely in this book. And the tax code's fluidity means the structural details will change slightly from year to year.

If you've never looked into any of these asset classes, I encourage you to choose the one that sounds most inviting to you and learn as much about it as possible.

Yes, you will face risks, and like anything worth doing, reaping the advantages will take some work, but you deserve to have all the benefits the wealthiest in the nation enjoy. Think about the things you could do with increased cash flow. Would you spend more time with your family? What dream could you fulfill? Whichever part of true wealth is most important to you, it's time to build a team that will win for you.

CHAPTER FOUR
BUILD A BUSINESS

Building a business might be the most lucrative way to increase your cash flow, save on taxes, and build an appreciating asset that can feed the other super asset classes. In fact, most significant wealth in this country has been accumulated by people who own businesses.

If you're starting a new endeavor and currently work a nine-to-five, I recommend keeping your day job until you get your business off the ground. One study revealed that businesses that begin as a side hustle are one-third less likely to fail. A side hustle gives you an opportunity to grow gradually and make mistakes.[3]

What Kind of Business Should I Start?

In his book, *Rich Dad, Poor Dad*, Robert Kiyosaki says, "Financial struggle is often the result of people working all their lives for someone else." Even if you love your job, there are significant tax advantages to starting your own business. Side hustles make for great beginnings. If you live in a populated area and have the passion, you might be a pet sitter, provide lawn care, or start a cleaning service. Technology has increased the types of business opportunities available. Online reselling has become a popular small business. People with specializations can tutor, trouble shoot, coach, counsel, develop apps, provide digital marketing or content creation services, or get into e-commerce. And all of this can be done remotely now.

These can all be relatively low-budget startups. No need for extravagant accessories to start. You can easily pick up a second-hand desk and even put books under your computer to make it a standing desk. Those with a bit of startup money or the ability to get a loan might look into franchise opportu-

> The key is finding a business that has scalability, dimension, or both.[IP]

nities or expanded ways to use your special talents.

The key is finding a business that has scalability, dimension, or both.[IP] For instance, you could start a granola bar business. Those low-cost items are often easier to scale and have low profit margins. You could sell hundreds and thousands of these snacks.

Unfortunately, no one will pay ten dollars for a granola bar, so it's difficult to find dimension (high-dollar profit margin). On the other hand, those who buy and sell Bugattis, expensive Italian cars, deal in products with great dimension. High profit margins mean you can sell much less in quantity while making tremendous profit. And if you can do both—sell a product or service that has scale and dimension—you live in the best of both worlds.

My nephew loves cars. He knows what to look for and knows a good deal when he sees it. He's become quite good at buying and selling cars online at a profit. This gives him greater cash flow, with business deductions, to help lower his taxes on the additional income from short-term capital gains. But buying and selling one car at a time makes for a side hustle, not a scalable business. Should he be able to find several every week and perhaps add an employee or utilize technology to help him locate buyers and sellers, it could turn into something more lucrative.

As you consider which business would be best for you, start by focusing on something society needs. Think about the times when you've heard someone say, "I wish there was a . . ." Can you provide that item? Or maybe you've said, "I never want to do that frustrating thing again." If you find a way to fix it so everyone who shares your frustration never has to do that frustrating thing again, you can make a profit. How do you think the first dishwasher came to be?

Your idea doesn't even have to be completely original. Many people have successfully started a business by improving on the invention and services of others. iPhones weren't the first cell phones, but the way they expanded on the innovation made the brand one of the hottest topics you come across today. Lawn mowers have existed for hundreds of years, but they got better when someone added a motor and another person decided we should ride. Most people thought it couldn't get any better until one innovator introduced the zero-turn mower to the market. What if the person who motorized the mower had decided, "We have a mower, I don't think I should try to improve on it"? Life would be more difficult, and someone would have missed out on all the profit.

One side note: Don't spend countless hours, days, or years, trying to find the "perfect" business. I would take an average idea I can execute effectively over the most phenomenal business idea any day. Execution is the key! Make sure you can move forward on your idea and are willing to put in the hours and commitment at the beginning.

> **I would take an average idea I can execute effectively over the most phenomenal business idea any day.**

After you find your executable business idea, consider its recession-proof status. If your passion is fitness or travel, a gym or travel agency might be the way to go. But if people lose their income or costs rise, they'll have to cut out discretionary expenses, and these types of businesses may suffer. So, sometimes it is best to keep your passion in an area for yourself, and start a business that will survive in all business environments.

You also don't want a business that owns you rather than the other way around. I've heard bakers talk about despising their passion because 4:00 a.m. comes way too early every day after staying up until midnight to take care of the bookkeeping. You need to put provisions in your business plan for practical things like hiring help or utilizing technology to take care of long hours.

You might also consider one of the many businesses that the government gives even greater tax advantages for—research and development and agriculture, for example. The key to taking advantage of every tax law is gaining knowledge. Read books, attend seminars, or find a mentor.

Building a business takes work. Lori Greiner of QVC and Shark Tank fame is attributed with one of my favorite quotes, "Entrepreneurs are willing to work eighty hours a week to avoid working forty hours a week." Be prepared to put in the time to execute! If starting a business is something you're passionate about, and you can see how it will increase your wealth across all areas, it will be worth it.

Leverage Other People's Money

Depending on the type of business you start, you may need to leverage OPM first. While, or after, utilizing your own resources, most people start with family or friends, loans, or other investors. These are the most basic means of using other people's money. Regarding family and friends, to avoid interfering with the wealth of those relationships, enter these OPM opportunities with extreme care and clearly signed agreements.

Taking advantage of tax laws also allows you to use OPM to grow your business, decrease your tax burden, and increase your cash flow. Business owners can deduct salaries, rent, office supplies, employee benefits, travel, and more. Even part of your home expenses might be deductible if they meet the IRS qualifications.

You must have an actual business, and the expenses must be ordinary business expenses that are necessary and documented. Both the self-employed entrepreneur and the one who employs a team can take advantage of the tax laws. However, the benefits offered to a business that creates jobs are even greater. For instance, if you allow your children to work in your business, they can earn that spending money you know they will be asking you for, and you can use the amount of their paycheck as part of your deductions.

Leverage Other People's Time

Many small businesses start out as lone ranger operations. As a self-employed individual, you control everything, but you also do all the work, making it difficult to scale—especially if you're still working a day job to make ends meet at home and funneling as much money as possible back into your business until it grows. And while employees might seem like an expense you can't afford, often leveraging OPT can speed growth.

When you find skilled individuals to combine with OPT leverage, you can scale your business quickly. The money you pay these people is deductible as well as advantageous. If one person can bring one hundred dollars an hour into the business, two can bring two hundred. If half of that goes into salary and benefits to pay for OPT, your business has at least doubled its net profit while avoiding taxes on the expenses it takes to generate the additional revenue. There can be negatives to adding human capital to your business. People bring their own "baggage" and potential human resources problems that you must deal with. That brings us to our next leverage—technology.

Leveraging Technology

Small businesses can now leverage an opportunity entrepreneurs fifty years ago didn't have. For example, many electronic point-of-sale programs and artificial intelligence strategies provide excellent business solutions. These technological advancements give you back hours of record keeping time and work for much less than someone willing to give you the same services technology provides.

Ask yourself, "Can I get the help I need by using technology that may allow the multiplication of my efforts without having to hire someone?" This allows you to avoid the potential cost and complexity human capital may bring. I have seen many successful businesses, like drop-shipping, employ only one person—you!

As you continue to grow, project management tools can help you streamline your business and allow your team to work more efficiently. Plus, customer relation management and email marketing software allow you to stay in touch with your clients with little effort on your part. The key is balancing technology with human resources to provide your business with the most economical and customer serving partnership possible.

Can you see the benefit of leveraging technology in your business? For example, suppose you integrate technology in your business that will help double your sales, and it costs $20,000. Not only will your business grow, but at a 40 percent tax rate, the government will pay you back $8,000 when you deduct your $20,000 technology investment! In the same way, should you choose to hire someone to help you double your sales, your new employee's $50,000 salary really only costs $30,000 when you factor in the tax savings. This is powerful stuff!

Power Plays

In each asset class, you'll find the standard tax savings tips like I mentioned above; however, most of these cash flow opportunities also have Power Plays. I don't want anyone to miss out on the advantages of the wealthy because they don't know the possibilities. For instance, many write-offs for businesses can work to your personal advantage.

Power Play 1: If you use your car for an LLC or corporation, you might be able to deduct some, most, or all of the expense of the vehicle's purchase.

Power Play 2: Likewise, if your business requires travel and you prefer to deduct mileage on your work vehicles, you can easily and legally work your family vacation around your business trips. This means you can deduct mileage and one hotel room, perhaps some meals, or even a plane ticket if you choose to fly. How would it feel to know your family vacation is actually reducing your tax burden?

Power Play 3: Small things like taking care of household errands on your way to a business meeting, for instance, trips to the post office or visiting a client, can be implemented strategically. Now, your personal mileage is included in your write-off mileage.

Power Play 4: Depending on how your business is structured and how much income you have, you may be able to take advantage of *qualified business income* (QBI) deductions.

Chapter 4

Power Play: Buying/Leasing A Car as a
W2 Employee vs. a Business Owner

Deductions	Business Owner	W2 Employee
Oil, Gas, Repairs & Tires	✔	
Insurance	✔	
Registration Fees	✔	
Licenses	✔	
Depreciation/ Lease Payments	✔	
Registration Fees	✔	

The Strategy: Try To Make Every Trip A Business Trip

Even the smallest business can take advantage of these Power Plays. Whether you're turning your hobby into a side hustle for cash flow or embarking on an entirely new adventure, becoming an entrepreneur can increase your income, give you more opportunities to use the tax code to your benefit, and potentially provide freedom from the nine-to-five.

CHAPTER FIVE
THE WORLD OF REAL ESTATE

Business endeavors are not the only way to take advantage of beneficial government policies. Significant wealth has been created in this country by investing in real estate. One advantage to this investment is that even when real estate prices go down, they never drop to zero. Actually, housing prices increased an average of 5 percent a year between 1968 and 2009[4], and from 1978 through 2022, commercial property averaged an annual return of more than nine percent.[5]

There are multiple ways to invest in real estate. Investors can flip homes. You've probably seen those men and women on HGTV who purchase a property, fix it up, and then resell for a profit. Some invest strictly for the capital gain they make when they sell. Other investors get into real estate for cash flow.

Some even invest in high-appreciating areas and take a negative cash flow hoping for a higher price in the future. I prefer the growth *and* positive cash flow. That is what I recommend you focus on, and it's the area I'll describe in this section.

To create cash flow through real estate, you'll either need up-front capital, OPM, or some creative financing. Fortunately, most traditional lenders only require 20–25 percent down on real estate. In addition to the property's appreciation, real estate has the potential for rental income attached to it, allowing you to create regular cash flow to pay the mortgage, take care of maintenance, and even pay yourself; all while utilizing the leverage of OPM.

Types of Real Estate

There are two main types of real estate to concentrate on, commercial and residential. Both can provide substantial rental income and appreciation opportunities.

Residential real estate provides a place for people to live, making it attractive for the government to give incentives. Whether it's a single-family dwelling, a duplex, a multi-family residence, or an entire apartment complex, all the expenses related to creating cash flow, except the land, are deductible. And low-income housing offers even greater tax credits.

Commercial property investments often have larger acquisition costs, but the rental income has more potential as well. Plus, this type of property most often has a triple net lease, meaning the lessee pays for all expenses except the mortgage. This can be as simple as a single small building housing a coffee shop or an accountant's office, or as large as a multi-office building, a plaza, a hi-rise, storage units, a data center, or any place someone might house a business. Deductions fall in the same categories as residential real estate. Additionally, the government may offer even more tax benefits for commercial real estate. I encourage you to stay current with tax legislation for items like bonus depreciation for even bigger write-offs.

While these tax savings make real estate an attractive way to increase cash flow, this super asset class has an additional tax credit unique to this investment area.

The Magic of Depreciation

All real estate, other than the purchase of a private home, offers a phantom annual deduction called depreciation. While some assets in your standard business are depreciable, real estate depreciation may even be more substantial.

The size of your depreciation deduction depends on the type of real estate and the purpose of the depreciable item. However, before you can figure depreciation, you have to divide

> While some assets in your standard business are depreciable, real estate depreciation may even be more substantial.

your investment into four categories: land, buildings, improvements, and contents. For instance, a residential real estate building is eligible for depreciation over twenty-seven and a half years, while a commercial building is depreciated over thirty-nine years.

Let's say Justin is in a 40 percent federal and state marginal tax bracket, and he purchased a piece of commercial real estate for $1.7 million. He used $500,000 from his ordinary or W2 income for the down payment and made $300,000 in improvements to increase the value of his investment to $2,000,000. To cover the improvements and the initial purchase, he borrowed $1,500,000 from the bank. The land value of $200,000 doesn't qualify for depreciation; everything else is eligible.

The $400,000 he detailed in the purchase agreement for contents will be depreciable. Justin made sure things like window treatments, furniture, window air conditioners and the like were all listed in the agreement so he wouldn't have to pay for a cost segregation study after the sale. Though they're depreciable over a three- to seven-year period, we'll use the average of five years for the contents depreciation deduction. This means Justin will have a deduction of $80,000 a year for five years on contents.

Next, Justin will depreciate $300,000 worth of improvements over the next fifteen years, things like landscaping, fencing, outdoor lights, and awnings that were added to improve the property. His improvements deduction will be about $20,000 each year.

With the categories defined, Justin now has $1,100,000 of the total value in the building. His CPA will divide that by thirty-nine, adding a little more than $28,000 to his annual depreciation deduction.

Let's assume Justin will see a 12 percent cash on cash return from his investment. Since he invested $500,000 cash, he can estimate an annual cash flow of $60,000 per year after all expenses are paid including the mortgage.

Justin seemed pretty happy to find out he could take a total depreciation deduction of $128,000 against passive income—such as rent. This means the rental income is completely tax free, and he still has an additional $68,000 in depreciation he can write off against other passive income! Do you see what Justin did? He converted ordinary income into an investment that now has passive income and large tax deductions that make the cash flow tax free. You should have seen his face when his wealth advisor told him the current tax law allowed him to have even bigger deductions.

Purchase of a $2 Million Commercial Building with $500,000 Down Payment				
Building Components	Percent of Bldg	Value	Depreciation Time	Yr 1 Depreciation
Land	10%	$200,000	Cannot Depreciate	$0
Bulding itself	55%	$1,100,000	39 years	$28,205
Improvements	15%	$300,000	15 years	$20,000
Building Contents	20%	$400,000	3-7 yrs (assume 5)	$80,000
		$2,000,000		**$128,205**

A quick aside: Every CPA is now thinking that my depreciation calculation is not accurate, and they would be correct. Let me explain. This is an investment book more than a tax guide. The actual way to calculate depreciation in the first year is much more complex based on when the property is put into service. I am assuming full depreciation in the first year to make the concept easier to understand. In almost all situations, there are rules like mid-month convention or mid-year convention that govern when you start depreciating. Thanks IRS for making this easy.

For example, if you made your purchase on January 1 and the building was in service on January 1, you would probably use mid-month convention and get 11.5 months worth of depreciation. If purchased and put into service in October, you would probably use mid-year convention and get 6 months of depreciation in the first year. For the rest of the book, I will continue calculating depreciation as I did in the example, however I cannot stress enough the importance of having a team of qualified advisors guiding you as you begin building your portfolio. Back to Justin and his bigger deductions.

In the year Justin bought the building, improvements and contents could be depreciated at 60 percent the first year because of government legislation that allowed for bonus depreciation. This took his first year depreciation deduction on his new real estate from the $128,205 we see in the chart to nearly $450,000. That $500,000 he used for a down payment would have been taxed at 40 percent. But now, rather than paying $170,000 in taxes, he could potentially owe very little on that portion of his income if structured properly (see Power Play 2 at the end of the chapter).

Depreciation of Commercial Real Estate				
Breakdown of Components for Depreciation	Value	% of Building	Depreciation Time/Years	Allowable Depreciation Year 1
Land (Cannot Depreciate)	$200,000	10%	None	$0
Bulding itself	$1,100,000	55%	39	$28,205
Improvements	$300,000	15%	15**	$180,000
Building Contents	$400,000	20%	3-7 (avg 5)**	$240,000
Total Cost of Original Build	$2,000,000			**60% Yr. One Depreciation in 2024
Total Year One Depreciation				**$448,205**

Once again, the IRS makes this more complicated. In reality, when you take bonus depreciation, you still get to take your regular depreciation. To make the math and the concept easier to digest, I am only utilizing the bonus depreciation in these calculations.

More Benefits When You Sell Your Real Estate

When you decide to sell your real estate, even more tax advantages kick in. Suppose Justin's commercial real estate investment increases by about 3 percent per year and his cash flow grows at a rate of 4 percent. Fast forward seven years, and in addition to the appreciation in value, his annual income for the property is now almost $79,000 per year. The rental income has paid off about $150,000 of the mortgage balance, bringing it to $1,350,000. And he has written off hundreds of thousands of dollars of depreciation against passive income saving hundreds of thousands in income tax. If Justin sells his property for $2,500,000, he will have total sales proceeds of $1,112,000 after he pays off the mortgage—a nice jump from his original $500,000 investment.

But what about the $500,000 profit on his real estate deal as well as the depreciation he deducted? If this were ordinary income, Justin would pay 40 percent in taxes on that half million, but the IRS calls this long-term capital gains. Rather than 40 percent, he will pay taxes at the lower capital gains rate, which for him currently will be a total of 23.8 percent at the federal level, and 3 percent at the state level. He will also need to pay depreciation recapture on the dollars he depreciated; however, this is taxed at a special rate of 25 percent. Remember, he would have had to pay 40 percent (37 percent federal and 3 percent state) on that amount if he hadn't written off the depreciation against his income every year.

Now, when Justin pays the recapture tax, it will be at a maximum federal tax rate of 25 percent, and using the same 3 percent state tax rate, he will pay only 28 percent instead of 40 percent. All in, Justin's $700,000 in depreciation along with the $500,000 in capital gains means he will pay a total of $330,000 in long-term capital gains taxes and recapture. Rather than the $480,000 he would have paid at a 40 percent rate.

Sale of a Commercial Building			
Original Purchase Price	Growth Rate	Value after 7 years	Amount remaining on Mortgage
$2,000,000	3%	$2,459,747	$1,346,849.80
	Total Sales Proceeds		
	$1,112,897.20		
Scenario One	Amount	Tax Rate	Taxes
Capital Appreciation	$500,000	26.8%	$134,000
Depreciation Recapture	$700,000	28%	$196,000
		Total:	$330,000
Scenario Two	Amount	Tax Rate	Taxes
Ordinary Income	$1,200,000	40%	$480,000

Not only did his real estate investment give him seven years of cash flow, the depreciation schedule gave him big tax savings, and when he sold it, he saved another big chunk in the difference between the tax on regular income and capital gains.

But there's another option with even more savings. Justin's friend Brit invests in real estate and also took advantage of the depreciation deduction to avoid paying taxes on her capital gains. Brit's wealth advisor suggested she take advantage of a *1031 exchange.*

So, when Brit sold her building and made a $500,000 profit, she purchased a piece of property on the other side of town with potential for higher rental income. This means she increased her cash flow without paying taxes on the gain.

Brit originally invested in a four-unit apartment building at $2,000,000 with a $500,000 down payment. By the time she was ready to sell, she had paid about $150,000 on the mortgage, and the building had increased in value by $500,000. Rather than pay capital gains and depreciation recapture like Justin did on $1,200,000, Brit used the sales proceeds of $1,112,000 as a 25 percent down payment on her next, larger investment property.

Brit Buys a Building with $500,000 Downpayment

1st 1031

Original Purchase Price	Growth Rate	Value after 7 years
$2,000,000	3%	$2,459,747
	Amt remaining on Mortgage $1,346,850	Total Sales Proceeds $1,112,897
2nd Building Purchase $4,450,000	25% Down Payment $1,112,897	12% Cash on Cash Return $133,547

2nd 1031

2nd Bldg Orig Price	Growth Rate	Value after 7 years
$4,450,000	3%	$5,472,938
	Amt remaining on Mortgage $2,596,352	Total Sales Proceeds $2,876,586
3rd Building Purchase $11,506,344	25% Down Payment $2,876,586	12% Cash on Cash Return $345,190

To activate the 1031 exchange, she has to invest in a new piece of property of the same value or greater, and she must replace the value of the debt that was currently on the building. So, she found a building valued at $4,450,000. Brit secured a mortgage with a 6 percent interest rate. Between that and the anticipated 12 percent cash on cash return, Brit will see an annual income on this building of $133,500 each year, all while paying $0 in capital gains taxes or depreciation recapture. The 1031 exchange allows her to defer those.

What if Brit repeats the process in seven years? The net proceeds from her apartment building will be about

$2,876,000. Using that amount for the down payment, Brit will be able to purchase a third investment property valued at $11,500,000. The annual cash-on-cash return at the same 12 percent rate will be approximately $345,000. In 14 years, she moved from an annual cash flow of $60,000 to $345,000! And, because she used another 1031 exchange, she did not pay any capital gains tax or recapture this time either. With depreciation, she will avoid paying tax on most or all of her passive income for a long time. There are additional rules to successfully complete a 1031 exchange so please consult your advisor before undertaking.

Perhaps you're thinking, "I don't have $500,000 to get started. There's no way I can get a loan for $1.5 million." Don't get hung up on the numbers. The strategy remains the same even if you begin with a less expensive, single-family dwelling.

Extra Real Estate Opportunities

Regardless of which real estate opportunity you choose, you'll need to do your research to be certain you're applying the most current tax laws. That 60 percent depreciation I mentioned on improvements and contents is in effect this year, but it changes annually.

Current legislation also unlocked tax benefits for investing in distressed economic areas. Approximately 18 percent of the United States has been designated opportunity zones. These struggling areas need more stores, restaurants, and housing. The government believes offering tax incentives for those willing to put money into these depressed areas will result in economic growth and job creation. To that end, additional tax incentives are given to investors in these areas. Plus, if you hold that opportunity zone property for at least ten years, you might be able to permanently exclude taxes on the investment gains when sold. To participate, you must invest money on which you would have had to pay capital gains tax from a previous sale within 180 days.

Real estate offers some of the most advantageous Power Plays. By implementing as many as possible, this asset class can put you in a very good position for minimizing taxes while maximizing cash flow.

Power Plays

 **Power Play 1**: As you might have guessed, the 1031 exchange is your first major real estate Power Play. By continually reinvesting, you can keep your cash flow growing and minimize the tax burden on your growing investment.

 **Power Play 2**: While the depreciation deduction is available only when applied to passive income for the average individual, real estate professionals can take those phantom deductions against *all* their income. To be a professional does not mean you need a real estate license. A professional must be acquiring, managing, developing, and researching real estate, working at least 750 hours a year (this number could change at any time) in real estate. If you or your spouse meet the requirements of a professional, you can take advantage of this powerful strategy and deduct even more of your phantom depreciation. Check the rules to make sure you can achieve

this status and take advantage of the write-offs against not only passive, but active—or ordinary—income.

Power Play 3: If you enjoy traveling, you might invest in rental property near your favorite vacation spot. Every time you visit your real estate, you can write off your travel expenses, even if it includes a trip to the beach.

Power Play 4: If you have rental property as well as another entrepreneurial venture, be sure to rent from yourself. You lower the taxes for your business endeavor when you pay rent, but because you pay yourself, you aren't losing the money. Additionally, depreciation will offset much of the rent your rental company receives.

Power Play 5: Find a tax professional who fully understands the most current tax laws. For instance, the current law allows you to depreciate 60 percent on your improvements and contents. While that huge amount is only available now, similar tax laws are passed on a regular basis. You want to take advantage of every single one.

Power Play 6: You may be able to defer or reduce the tax on your capital gains by taking advantage of opportunity zones. You might use capital gains from a variety of areas (e.g., real estate, stocks, sale of a business, etc.) to invest in those distressed areas.

CHAPTER SIX
CAPITALIZING ON OIL AND NATURAL GAS

Almost everyone has heard of energy tax credits, but few actually use them to their fullest potential. Right now, incentives for renewable energy are available through the federal government and most state governments. They offer credits for installing solar panels on your house or business, not to mention, you lower your gas or electric bill. Still, I recommend doing your homework or consulting an informed professional to see whether the savings balance the cost of the product.

Maybe you or someone you know has already applied renewable energy tax credits and discovered tax incentives for residential property. Even commercial property can often take advantage of these kinds of improvements. However, with the voracity that the world consumes energy, renewable energy, while a part of the solution, cannot meet the demand.

We Need Energy

Despite the move toward these clean energy sources, we still need traditional sources, and the oil and gas industry offers even more in tax savings and Power Plays. Solar and wind energy get a lot of press these days; regardless, our world isn't yet ready to turn off fossil fuel feeds. In fact, factories in Germany were all set to abandon fossil fuels by 2022. In October of that year, one of the largest factories in the country faced the hard facts and pushed back its clean energy goals by eight years.[6]

Scientists are working on ways to make nuclear energy more affordable and efficient. They're studying past failures to expedite the transition. Still, we are years away from full implementation. Hydroelectric looks like a good alternative—until we have a dry year and the water flow fluctuates too much to keep up.

Let's face it. We enjoy our lights, hot showers, air conditioners, and other modern conveniences. Electronics touch every aspect of our life now. Because of our dependence on everything that moves us, brings us information, and makes our lives more comfortable, the United States is on the verge of maxing out our current energy supply. Some of the problem stems from decreased production around the world. Europe already faces blackouts. In the winter of 2022, they were burning paper and wood to keep warm.

Add the increasing demand AI computing puts on the energy infrastructure, and we have a recipe for brownouts across our country, particularly in highly populated areas.[7] As you can imagine, this is something the government wants to avoid.

Exorbitant renewable energy costs and the fact that even alternative energy sources currently depend on oil and gas means our reliance on these two energy sources isn't going to disappear anytime soon.

Oil and Gas Ownership

Oil and gas drilling projects are currently one of the best tax shelters in the United States for accredited investors. There are income and/or net worth requirements, but it might be worth reviewing them to see if you qualify. Despite their advantages, many tax professionals and wealth advisors have limited knowledge regarding this investment. The staff at Harvest Advisors find themselves educating even CPAs on the strategies of oil and gas.

One accountant called me quite close to the April 15 deadline not long ago, "I see some write-offs you think our client should take, but those aren't allowed." I explained that even though the government took away the ability to deduct passive losses against active income in other areas, they left special treatment for oil and gas. I cited the IRS code and alleviated the tax professional's concern.

> One advantage oil and gas has over real estate is the ability to write off passive losses against active income.

One advantage oil and gas has over real estate is the ability to write off passive losses against active income. Prior to 1987, real estate shared this trait, but another thing you must look out for when you're playing this game with the wealthy is the IRS's power to rewrite the code anytime they see fit. Fortunately, oil and gas investments have maintained this Power Play.

If you're dealing with oil and gas at any level, even if you're simply bringing in a few hundred a month from mineral rights your ancestors left your family, ask your accountant if they are familiar with the tax landscape and deductions on oil and gas. If done incorrectly, it has the potential to ruin your write-offs in that area. So, let's break down some of the ways you can increase cash flow and maximize tax write-offs through oil and gas. Before we begin, remember, like with any investment, there are risks investing in oil and gas. As you research this area, please review the risk profile.

First, assuming you are not going to personally hire petroleum engineers and drilling rigs to go on the search for black gold, you could become a *general partner* (GP) in a drilling program. The United States has a tremendous number of oil and gas drilling companies popping up, and they all need investors. Before you put money into one of them, you need to be sure the company has an excellent long-term track record, more than adequate insurance protection, and, one thing I find very important, has never been sued. Especially if you're new to the oil and gas area, you don't want a rookie oilman at the helm of your investment. I would even avoid an experienced oilman starting his or her own drilling company.

The partial ownership aspect of being a GP offers several options for deductions. The first year, some of the machinery that is required to drill, plus the intangible drilling costs (IDCs)—those that offer no value after completion, like ground clearing and survey work—are completely deductible. This can create an offset of up to 80–90 percent of your ordinary income.

Once production begins, investors begin to see cash flow, usually within three to six months, and they may see income for up to a couple of decades, though they're likely to see most of their cash flow in the first three to five years. In most instances, because the oil and gas are being depleted as they are removed from the ground, nearly everyone receiving cash flow will also receive a depletion allowance of at least 15 percent each year. So, only 85 percent of your oil and gas income is taxable. For example, if you receive $80,000 in cash flow from your investment, you'll start with only about $68,000 of taxable income. And wait until you see the Power Play if you choose to reinvest your tax savings!

Chapter 6

Investing As A General Partner

Oil & Gas Drilling Investment	$200,000
Original Taxes Owed	($80,000)
Income Tax Owed (Assuming 90% write-off)	($8,000)
Income Tax Savings	$72,000

Depletion Allowance	
1st Year Income	$80,000
15% Depletion Allowance	($12,000)
Taxable Ordinary Income	$68,000

Suppose Justin decided to put money into an oil and gas drilling program as a GP. Usually drilling programs invest in multiple wells. For example, some invest in as few as three wells, but the number may be upwards to several dozen. By investing in multiple wells, Justin spreads out some of his risk.

Let's assume Justin put $200,000 into a drilling program as a GP and is in a 40 percent income tax bracket (37 percent federal and 3 percent state). Most states allow deductions, but a few do not. As we mentioned, he may be able to write off up to 90 percent of the investment in the first year. Before the investment, Justin would have paid $80,000 in income taxes on this $200,000 of ordinary income. His investment in this oil and gas drilling program reduces that to $8,000 in income taxes. Plus, he has a full $200,000 investment in the drilling program. What could you do with an additional $72,000 in tax savings?

Other Oil and Gas Opportunities

Limited Partnerships

Investing into a drilling program as a limited partner may work well for those who want to invest but don't want the risk of being a general partner. As a limited partner, you do not get to benefit from the write-offs against ordinary income like a general partner, but you still get the cash flow, and you still receive the depletion allowance which reduces your ordinary income tax.

Oil and Gas Mineral Rights

Investing in property with mineral rights can be another avenue for increased cash flow. This is usually the least risky form of investing in oil and gas. Those who own the mineral rights lease their property to a drilling company and receive income when the well(s) produces. Since you aren't footing the bill for drilling, you have less to lose, but you also do not receive the IDC write-offs.

Oil and Gas in Retirement Accounts

You may invest in oil and gas in your retirement accounts and have the cash flow from the investment flow back into your retirement account. Typically, these are not partnership units, but Limited Liability Corporation shares. The different structure keeps partnership units out of your retirement accounts and avoids potential *unrelated business taxable income* (UBTI). Don't worry, the drilling program or your advisor can navigate this for you. Wait until you see Power Play 3 at the end of this chapter for a way to unleash a great strategy.

Oil and Gas Opportunity Zones

Another phenomenal investment opportunity under the current legislation is the Opportunity Zone. Remember, like we discussed in the real estate section, Qualified Opportunity Zones (QOZ) are areas determined to be in economic distress and are eligible for specific tax benefits with capital gains. Approximately 18 percent of the land in the US, according to the US Treasury Department, is in QOZs.[8] These zones were designed to spur economic growth and job creation in distressed areas. Most people who are familiar with QOZs associate them with real estate investing, but you can invest in oil and gas in a QOZ as well. A Qualified Opportunity Fund (QOF) allows you to invest into QOZs and receive the tax benefits.

Investors have 180 days after realizing a capital gain (from real estate, stock, land, etc.) to invest the capital gain portion into a QOF. What benefits do you receive?

- Current laws allow for Capital Gains Tax Deferral and Reduction. The most recent bill requires you to pay capital gains tax on only 90 percent of your original capital gain or on the value of the investment, whichever is less at that time.

- Passive Income from the Investment.

- Reinvestment of Excess Revenue into Additional Assets (oil and gas production.)

- Tax Free Gains After Ten Years: After holding for ten years, if the QOF is sold you will pay no capital gains tax on the gain in the investment.

I believe oil and gas can even be more powerful in a QOF than real estate because of the potential for lowering your tax owed in 2027. Remember the IDCs and write-offs from the drilling program? These "costs" lower the value of the investment and can potentially lower your capital gains tax owed. This is an incredible opportunity if you have capital gains and nowhere to shelter them.

Oil and gas investing can be a powerful way to increase your cash flow and decrease your taxes, and there are so many opportunities available. Again, these investments carry risk. Please familiarize yourself with it. I strongly urge you to get assistance from a financial professional. On the other hand, if your advisor simply dismisses oil and gas as too risky without listing the pros and cons, they probably don't fully understand the opportunities. In this case, a second opinion could prove invaluable.

> Oil and gas investing can be a powerful way to increase your cash flow and decrease your taxes.

Power Plays

Power Play 1: You can use a 1031 exchange to invest in oil and gas mineral rights. Because these rights are recorded at the county level as real property, you can go back and forth between oil and gas and traditional real estate. For example, if you are going to sell real estate and cannot identify other real estate options, oil and gas mineral rights may be a solution to preserve your gains.

Power Play 2: Use an oil and gas drilling program to reduce taxes in a year where you may receive a large bonus, payout, or ordinary (W2) income. For example, let's assume you are receiving a compensation payout because the performance of your company was excellent. If you receive $300,000 and are in the 40 percent tax bracket already, you will pay $120,000 in taxes if you do nothing. If you invest the $300,000 into a drilling program, and we assume you can write off 90 percent of the investment in the first year, you would save $108,000 in taxes and still have the full $300,000 investment.

Power Play 3: Use your traditional tax-deferred IRA to buy into oil and gas drilling. Then in year two, convert it to a Roth IRA. When you convert a traditional IRA to a Roth, you pay taxes based on your highest current tax bracket. However, because of the deductions and IDCs, the value of your drilling program may decrease to only $15,000 in year two. If you put $100,000 from your IRA into oil and gas, in year two, the value on that investment may only be about $15,000. Then, when you take that $100,000 investment and move it to a Roth, you'll only pay taxes on the value of the investment ($15,000) rather than $100,000. And the cash flow from your $100,000 investment will be going into your Roth and will also be income-tax free in the future due to the nature of Roth IRAs.

CHAPTER SEVEN
PAPER ASSETS

Almost everyone is familiar with paper assets, and even those who dive deep into the other super assets classes have a portfolio full of paper. People have been investing in stocks since the early 1600s when the Dutch East India Company first sold interest in their transport business and paid dividends to their investors. It took nearly two hundred years for the concept to reach the Americas. That's when a group of merchants started meeting daily to buy and sell stocks, eventually creating the New York Stock Exchange.[9] Honestly, although most significant wealth in this country has been built through real estate and businesses, paper assets undergirded the growth. These cash infusions have been providing capital for the largest companies for a couple of centuries.

Stock and Bonds

Though we still call them paper assets, the exchange of most stocks and bonds takes place digitally today. Your financial investment in stocks gives you actual equity in the issuing company. You hold ownership in the business. Bonds, on the other hand, represent a claim on the underlying asset, more like a loan you make to a business or the government.

You can purchase paper assets in one of three environments—through a taxable account, an income-tax-deferred account, or an income-tax-free account.

If you're a W2 employee with benefits, you might participate in one of the latter two environments and not realize it. Qualified retirement plans, such as 401(k) s, 403bs, 457 plans, and others, along with traditional Individual Retirement Accounts (IRAs), fall into the income-tax-deferred environment. The full amount of your contribution is deductible in the year you contribute (with the exception of certain IRA contributions), and the growth is tax-deferred. You pay income taxes on these funds when you begin to make withdrawals after you retire.

The income-tax-free environment includes Roth IRAs, Roth Qualified Retirement Plans, and municipal bonds. In this environment, for the Roth plans, you pay taxes when you deposit the funds into your retirement account. The main benefit comes when you withdraw the funds. After years of growth, every penny remains income-tax free when you start taking distributions.

Depending on conditions your employer puts on your qualified retirement plan, you might be able to direct the funds into less traditional investments, much like the Power Play we discussed in the oil and gas section. Regardless of where you hold your retirement savings, it's a good idea to have an experienced advisor guide you.

The final environment is one most people don't think about, but fewer W2 employees take advantage of. Regardless of your income level, you can take advantage of a personal brokerage account. In this environment, taxes are pretty straightforward—you pay taxes on your portfolio income as well as realized capital gains.

Everyone should take advantage of any employer matching contributions into their retirement plans. But if you want to leverage the benefits the wealthy use to grow their income and lower their taxes, consider holding paper assets in all three environments. As you explore the many avenues of paper assets, you'll find the potential for special trading status and a variety of other ways to supercharge your retirement.

Paper Assets as a Business

For instance, if paper assets intrigue you, you might want to step into the realm of making paper assets a business. Professional traders typically track market data to identify patterns and trends— we call this technical analysis—rather than

> The key to becoming a professional trader is knowledge.

simply using fundamental analysis—examining a company's financials.

The key to becoming a professional trader is knowledge. Before you dive in head first, you need to explore the waters. Just like any other business, paper trading requires extensive research, education, mentors, and time. Fortunately, as the internet grows, the means for learning expands. A number of reputable sites offer opportunities for growing your knowledge. I also recommend using one that allows you to practice trading without the risk of losing money.

One of the decisions you'll have to make when you delve into the business of investing is whether you want to focus on stocks, bonds, options, ETFs, or mutual funds—though I don't recommend mutual funds in this arena.

We already mentioned stocks and bonds above, so let's look at the other types of investments we can make. ETF's (Exchange Traded Funds) offer greater diversification. Unlike stocks and bonds that focus on one company or entity, ETFs are baskets of securities. And while they may be more diversified, like mutual funds, they have differences. First, mutual funds can only be bought and sold after the closing bell rings each day. ETFs can be traded as long as the market is open, like an individual stock.

Stock Options give you the flexibility of investing less cash up front to control the same amount of underlying security. But the leverage they offer can be riskier than owning the stock outright.

Stock options offer two basic types of investment opportunities—*call and put options.*

If you buy a call option, you have the right, but not an obligation, to purchase the stock during an agreed upon timeframe, usually up to three months, at an agreed upon price. However, the seller of the call option has an obligation to sell the stock to you if you choose to exercise your right to purchase.

Alternatively, a put option goes the other way. If you buy a put option, you have the right but not the obligation to sell stock during an agreed upon timeframe and price to the seller of the put option, should the owner of the stock act upon his right to sell the stock (you are "putting" the stock to someone else). In other words, the seller of the put option has an obligation to buy the stock from you if you choose to exercise.

Suppose Justin has been watching a stock trend, and he feels as though it has the potential to make a huge climb. If the stock is trading at $100 per share, he could purchase one hundred shares for $10,000. Alternatively, Justin purchases a call option for those one hundred shares. Instead of paying $100 per share, Justin pays $300 for one month to control 100 shares of stock. Because it's a short-term option, Justin could lose his entire $300 if the stock doesn't climb or pulls back during his contract period. However, if the price rises from $100 per share to $110 per share, Justin's option also goes up. In this scenario, Justin's option might rise from a value of $300 to $1000. The stock increased by 10 percent, but the option value increased by 233 percent. Leverage is at work here.

Justin could sell the option for a $700 profit, but what if he decided to exercise his right to purchase the stock? If he had the capital, Justin could purchase the stock for $100 per share (the contract strike price) and turn around and sell it on the same day for $110 per share. He could even opt to hold the stock if he thought it would continue to rise in value.

Most traders don't put in the extra effort to buy and sell the stock. Instead, they simply sell their option and walk away with the $700 profit.

The scenarios and possibilities for options are limitless. You can combine put and call Options to create *straddles, collars, butterfly spreads,* and *condors*—each having a unique advantage and disadvantage and every one offering opportunities to leverage risk and return. But before you enter this endeavor for yourself, it's vital to learn everything you can.

A third opportunity to leverage paper assets is futures contracts. Like options, this allows you to hedge your losses; however, futures contracts have a built-in obligation to buy and sell on both sides. Futures offer the potential for higher profits, but as with most paper assets, the increased opportunity comes with higher risks.

The paper asset business can be lucrative, and there are many powerful tools to help you leverage the market and make it work for you. However, like becoming an electrician or a pilot, this isn't something you can enter into lightly. You will need hours and hours of training and practice. Think of yourself as moving from student to apprentice to flying solo.

My favorite place to do "paper trades," practicing without spending or receiving any cash, is the thinkorswim platform. This Schwab-owned site and a host of others allow you to practice trading and put your learning into action before you begin to invest real money. Additionally, you'll find that many places like thinkorswim offer training videos and strategies to help you get started. Nothing is more important than doing your homework, getting solid advice, and practicing on paper before you actually buy and sell. Attempting to go it alone with just a cursory reading of the internet will be as dangerous as trying to fly a plane or handle electricity after reading a handbook.

For the General Investor

What if you love your nine-to-five and are passionate about what you do? Then you may be an Intrapreneur—a person who gets to innovate, design, and develop as an employee of a company you enjoy. You might not have the desire or the time to forge a path into the business world of paper assets or other super asset classes. Perhaps you're worried because your company has a defined pension plan that doesn't take advantage of other retirement options. That's okay! Even if you don't have time for real estate, starting your own business, or getting into oil and gas, you can still maximize your retirement savings, minimize your taxes, and see all your hard work pay off.

I love paper assets because of their ability to make big gains and excellent cash flow. But I have three pieces of timeless advice for all investors.

First, you have to recognize and remove the emotions of fear and greed. The stock market is the only place I know where people run when something goes on sale. When things start to drop, people let fear drive them. However, most often, I look at the big drops like a clearance sale at my favorite store.

> **You have to recognize and remove the emotions of fear and greed.**

Anything less than a 15 percent drop is sort of baked into the process. We expect the market to fluctuate. You could look at those small swings like coupons at the grocery store. But when stock prices begin to hit a 20–25 percent drop, we have to find boldness in the face of our fear and wisely take advantage of the opportunities.

On the other hand, we can't let greed push us into foolish choices. Greed causes investors to put money into "hot trends" or hold on to some things for too long, thinking they will never go down.

In my case, holding out for more cost me in the long run. When I was nine, President Jimmy Carter's brother became the spokesperson of his own beer company. The more colorful Carter leveraged his brother's fame and sold a great deal of his Billy Beer. Though not even a decade old, I collected beer cans, so my dad made sure I had two. When Billy Beer production stopped in 1978, the price of those cans sky-rocketed. One person offered me $500 for the pair of rare cans. Dad told me to hold out. He believed we would find an even higher price from someone else.

It turns out they were not so rare. Not long after the cans broke records for high sales, the president of some beer can collectibles group deemed the cans were not unique and did not deserve this lofty price. Overnight, my prize cans dropped to the value of tin, a few cents a pound. Greed stole $500 from a pre-teen boy in Indiana.

> Mutual funds and ETFs can sometimes lead to "diworsification" rather than diversification.

Fear can be useful to hedge our greed. But when we allow our trepidation to keep us from investing wisely or allow greed to run away unchecked and without rational analysis, we lose every time.[IP] Don't let fear or greed rob you of your best deals.

Second, we need to recognize that mutual funds and ETFs can sometimes lead to "diworsification" rather than diversification. Yes, it's good to diversify; however, if we over diversify, we end up with too many positions and miss taking advantage of the best players— "diworsification." You may pass on some of your best returns by playing in the mutual fund/ETF court exclusively, but stepping outside of funds and ETFs requires you to invest in yourself with education.

Finally, I know I've said it before, but I can not stress enough the importance of having a fee-only wealth advisor. A good fiduciary can help you avoid the emotional decisions and allow you to stay disciplined in your investing. My firm, Harvest Financial Advisors, is fairly unique in that we don't limit our investments to basket-type funds; we invest primarily in individual securities.

Often, you can move to individual stocks through your IRAs. Though 401(k)s are limited to the mutual fund sector, IRAs and Roth IRAs allow you to purchase individual stocks. You can open brokerage accounts and move money as you see fit. Also, some retirement plans allow you to open brokerage accounts under the plan name, letting you purchase individual securities or Exchange Traded Funds. You'll obviously have to do your homework or get advice from a professional you trust; however, this kind of investing can prove to be extremely profitable.

Most people realize the benefits of depositing the maximum allowable contribution into their 401(k)s and IRAs each year. But do you realize people in the highest tax bracket can save more than $27,000 in taxes if they max out their 401(k)s and company contributions? Additionally, if you're over fifty, you can make catch up contributions that can also reduce your tax burden. And between the ages of 60 and 63, you can make a "super" catch up contribution to your 401(k) of up to $11,250.

High-earning small business owners and the self-employed can supercharge their tax savings by creating their own defined benefits plan. There are actuarial calculations that set contribution limits; however, the maximum ends up being more than three times that of a W2 employee, producing greater than $100,000 in potential tax savings.

Private Equity

As you begin to put money into businesses in the stock world, you may run across companies that need investors; however, they are not yet traded publicly. Tech companies probably offer the most opportunities for private equity investments today, but you'll find them in nearly every area of business.

One private equity company that intrigued me marketed a special glass additive. When added to paint, it created the strongest, chip-free paint imaginable. In extrusion molding, the special glass took the deformity rate to zero, increasing profits. These kinds of genius startups offer opportunities for private investors every day.

Private equity investments have one of three end games. Some have a goal to grow to the point they can begin to pay out returns to their investors. These companies have to get pretty big to be able to pay back the original investment and then pay dividends as well.

Most companies want to eventually be able to sell, either as a publicly traded company or an outright sale or merger. These two options offer more cash flow for the investors when the business finally sells.

Investors must pay close attention to private equity opportunities. While the promised payout often looks amazing, the risk grows at the same rate as the anticipated return. For instance, in that special glass company, the president was embezzling funds that should have gone to investors. Other businesses have failed and never paid out returns. Research and advice are imperative.

Publicly traded investments have more oversight. The Securities and Exchange Commission highly regulates them. Private equity opportunities don't have the assurances you find in the public entities, and you will need to be an accredited investor to get involved.

A number of private equity deals come across my desk every year. But the truth is the deal is only as good as the paper it's written on. Even if all the pro forma numbers the company presents look good, there is no assurance they will play out as predicted. Ask questions, look for discrepancies. Have they turned a profit over the past few years? What's the net worth? How has the owner increased the value? In order to make money, companies need a strong sales and marketing team, so be sure to evaluate this part of the company.

If you choose to find one on your own, you might look into a private equity fund. People who research this area every day bundle the most promising opportunities. These funds might have ten, twelve, or fourteen companies in one deal. It provides the safety of diversification. If one company fails, you still have others on your side. And when one of those companies rises to its full potential, you can capitalize on being one of the early investors. For instance, Tesla and SpaceX both started as private equity opportunities.

I typically encourage clients to look for late-stage investments and a grouping of approximately fifteen to spread out your risk. Private equity provides more growth opportunities than cash flow. But it's an area that allows accredited investors to realize capital gain rather than ordinary income when the company is sold, giving significant tax savings.

What if your Uncle Joe starts a pizza shop and needs investors? If you believe in your uncle and trust him to do well, then only invest what you can afford to lose. Many startups look to friends and family to help them before they move into the private equity market, but you'll want your uncle to prove his ability to run his business before you put money into his endeavor. If he's already burned through his initial cash roll with little to show for it, it's better to be true to the friendship than the business offering.

Power of Compounding

The beautiful thing about all these investments is the way they can grow with the power of compounding. Brit started working at age twenty-five, earning $70,000 a year. Each year she put $7,000 into a Roth 401(k). Let's assume her company matches 3 percent of her salary giving her another $2,100 for a total contribution of $9,100 per year. At an average growth rate of 8 percent a year, when she retires at age sixty-five, she'll have more than $2,300,000 to withdraw as she needs it, for the most part tax free.

Employer contributions generally go into a traditional pre-tax 401(k). They can be placed into the Roth side, but your reported income will be increased by the amount of the contribution and you will pay income tax on the company match. But what would it look like if Brit doubled her Roth 401(k) savings? When you add that to the company match, her total savings would increase to $16,100 per year. At what age could she retire with the same amount of money? By increasing her annual contribution, she would reach $2,300,000 seven years earlier. If she waits until age sixty-five to retire, that seven additional years will increase her available retirement funds to more than

$4,000,000. And all of this assumes she never gets a raise. What would you do? Would you retire early to enjoy life or keep investing?

Investment Value

Saving $9,100/yr from age 25

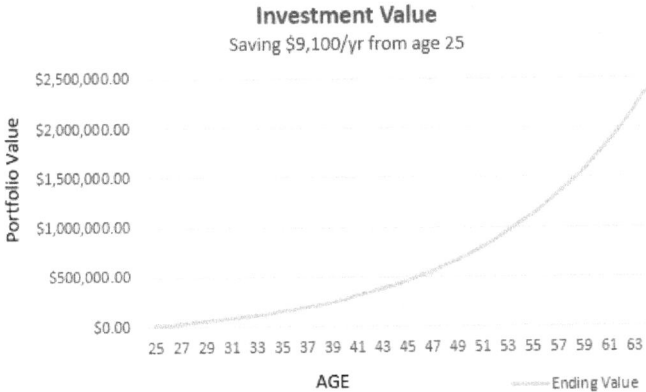

You probably aren't likely to stay at a job that doesn't give you a pay increase for forty years. Most people anticipate an annual raise. Let's assume Brit received a 3 percent raise each year. With a $9,100 annual

Investment Value

Saving $16,100/yr. from age 25

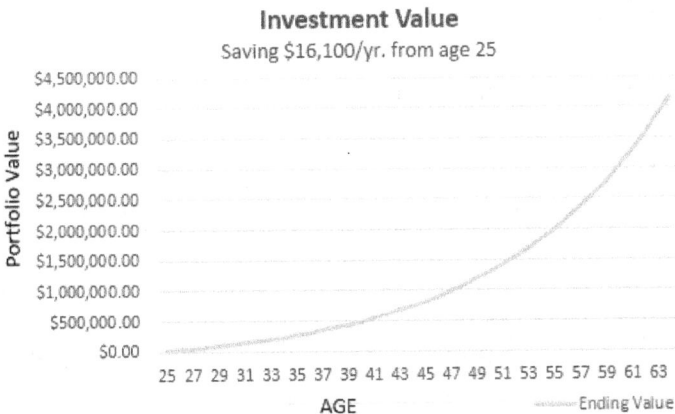

contribution, if she continues to increase her Roth 401(k) contributions by the same percentage and averages an 8 percent return, her efforts will reward her with more than $3,300,000 at age sixty-five. And if she doubled her annual contribution, her retirement accounts would total almost $6,000,000.

Investment Value by Age

Saving $9,100/yr with 3% increase/yr. from age 25

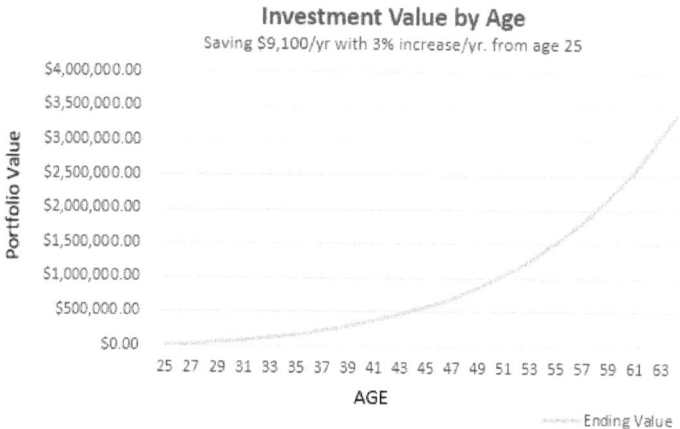

Ending Value

But what if that original amount of $2,300,000 satisfies you? Perhaps you don't need more than $3,000,000 when you retire. That $9,100 contribution increasing at 3 percent per year could allow you to retire at age sixty-one, and at $16,100, you could quit working as early as fifty-five. What could you do with ten extra years of freedom while you are still young and healthy enough to get around?

Some who read this may be worried because they zipped past age twenty-five fifteen years ago without the opportunity to make contributions to a qualified plan. Fortunately, it's never too late. If you start making contributions of $18,000 each year at age forty, and your employer matches at least $4,000, in twenty-five years, you will have about $1,700,000.

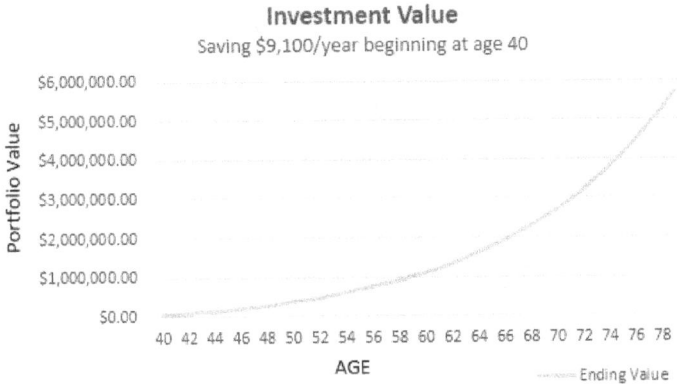

Investment Value

Saving $9,100/year beginning at age 40

Portfolio Value

$6,000,000.00
$5,000,000.00
$4,000,000.00
$3,000,000.00
$2,000,000.00
$1,000,000.00
$0.00

40 42 44 46 48 50 52 54 56 58 60 62 64 66 68 70 72 74 76 78

AGE   ──── Ending Value

Power Plays

Power Play 1: Becoming a trading professional is a Power Play of its own. While equity stock options are taxed based on the actual holding period, non-equity options, like commodities, futures, and broad-based indices, and futures contracts themselves, have an extra benefit. The gains on these types of options and futures are divided into 40 percent short term and 60 percent long term capital gains. This means 40 percent of your options and futures income will be taxed like regular income, while the other 60 percent will fall into a much more favorable tax schedule. Plus, when your trading moves to a full time job, before you pay the tax on that regular income, the IRS allows you to deduct your business expenses. The key here is to be sure you qualify as a professional under the IRS Tax Code. So double check with a professional before you begin to take these deductions.

Power Play 2: If you love your nine-to-five and don't want to move into professional status to take the extra tax advantages, you can do your trading in an IRA or a Roth IRA to maximize your tax savings.

Power Play 3: Combine ordinary income assets with capital gains assets to meet your cash flow needs but keep taxes down. For example, after you retire, let the cash flow from ordinary income sources like traditional IRAs and pensions fill up your lower tax brackets. When you reach the max for that lowest bracket, you can take distributions from taxable accounts—an amount that will not put you into the next, much higher income tax bracket, but will max out the amount you can claim under long-term capital gains rates. You could also pull from Roth IRAs to accomplish this. These funds won't put you in a higher income tax bracket because they are tax free. This could potentially save you a substantial amount in taxes each year.

Using Multiple Tax Environments In Retirement

Age	Annual Amount Withdrawn	Full amount taken from Pre-Tax IRA			$123,500 Taken from Pre-Tax IRA and $36,500 from Brokerage Account				
		Ordinary Income Tax	Cumulative Taxes		Fully Fund 12% Tax Bracket Only	Capital Gains Tax on Remainder*	Total Taxes Paid	Cumulative Tax	Cumulative Savings
65	$160,000.00	$18,882.00	$18,882.00		$10,852	$2,737.50	$13,589.50	$13,589.50	$5,292.50
66	$160,000.00	$18,882.00	$37,764.00		$10,852	$2,737.50	$13,589.50	$27,179.00	$10,585.00
67	$160,000.00	$18,882.00	$56,646.00		$10,852	$2,737.50	$13,589.50	$40,768.50	$15,877.50
68	$160,000.00	$18,882.00	$75,528.00		$10,852	$2,737.50	$13,589.50	$54,358.00	$21,170.00
69	$160,000.00	$18,882.00	$94,410.00		$10,852	$2,737.50	$13,589.50	$67,947.50	$26,462.50
70	$160,000.00	$18,882.00	$113,292.00		$10,852	$2,737.50	$13,589.50	$81,537.00	$31,755.00
71	$160,000.00	$18,882.00	$132,174.00		$10,852	$2,737.50	$13,589.50	$95,126.50	$37,047.50
72	$160,000.00	$18,882.00	$151,056.00		$10,852	$2,737.50	$13,589.50	$108,716.00	$42,340.00
73	$160,000.00	$18,882.00	$169,938.00		$10,852	$2,737.50			
74	$160,000.00	$18,882.00	$188,820.00		$10,852				
75	$160,000.00	$18,882.00	$207,702.00						
76	$160,000.00	$18,882.00	$22						
77	$160,000.00	$18,882							
78	$160,000								
79	$1								

This chart assumes:

- Married Filing Jointly with a standard deduction of $29,200

- 50% of brokerage account distribution is cost basis

- Capital gains rate is 15% and applies to half of revenue taken

- Ordinary income taxed as follows:

  ◊ Up to $29,000 = 0%

  ◊ Next $23,200 = 10%

  ◊ Next $71,100 = 12% (Total of $123,500 taxed at 12% or less)

  ◊ Over $123,500 = 22%

Let's assume you want $160,000 each year to live on, and you take the standard married filing jointly deduction—currently $29,200. By taking the entire amount from your pre-tax IRA account, you will pay $18,882 in federal income taxes. The first portion you withdraw is taxed at 10 percent, and the next portion is taxed at 12 percent. However, after you cross that third line—currently $94,300—everything over that amount jumps into the 22 percent bracket.

If you simply reduce the withdrawal from your pre-tax IRA by $36,500, lowering your total from those funds, and take that amount from a personal brokerage account instead, you'll pay long term capital gains tax on that final amount—currently 15 percent, and could save up to $5,300 in taxes assuming half of your brokerage account distribution is original cost basis.

Power Play 4: Have retirement savings in all three categories—income tax free, income tax deferred, and personal brokerage accounts. Unfortunately, the government can change the rules on the taxes on these funds any time they want to. They've even been known to add excise taxes to excess IRA distributions in the past. By having your retirement funds in all three areas, you can change withdrawal strategies if the IRS decides to switch up the tax situation on one or more of the categories we discussed in Power Play 3.

Power Play 5: A qualified retirement plan offers a potential all its own. We call it the Super or Mega Roth IRA. Suppose you've made the maximum allowed retirement plan contributions, including employer contributions and catch-up, to your traditional or Roth 401(k). In that case, we recommend you fully fund your Roth IRA if possible. If you have extra funds to add to your savings and your plan allows after-tax, non-Roth contributions, you might be able to supercharge your retirement savings. Your employer plan has to allow this supercharge in savings, and there are a few twists and turns along the way; however, if you make it to the end of the labyrinth, you can roll over your after-tax contributions to a Roth IRA outside of the plan giving you more investment opportunities and greater access to your money. A fee-only advisor can help guide you through this maze. Monica Dwyer, a fellow Certified Financial Planner Professional and one of my colleagues, created a great graphic to help our clients understand the Super Roth IRA. You can follow it to get a clearer picture of how to use this Power Play. If you'd like a larger version, you can visit our website to download. I've also included a list of questions in the Appendix that you can ask your plan provider to see if you qualify for the Super Roth.

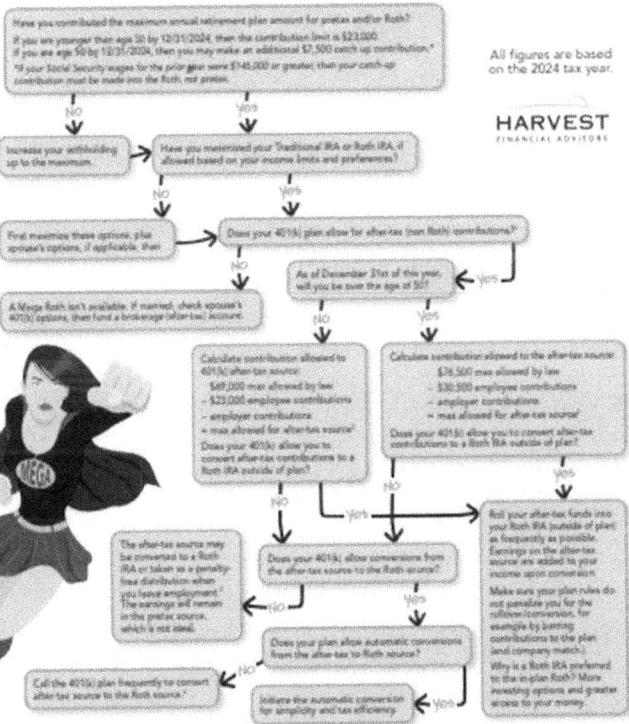

CHAPTER EIGHT
OTHER COMMODITIES

While there are many types of commodities—for instance, corn, wheat, and cotton—we are going to focus on precious metals to make up our fifth asset class. Unlike the other four, this asset class doesn't provide the cash flow you find in stocks, oil and gas, real estate, and owning a business. Plus, it doesn't offer the tax savings or Power Plays the other four super asset classes afford. As a side note, I would throw cryptocurrency into this bucket.

This asset class also has no fundamental analysis to determine what the true value should be. Like antiques and collectibles, commodities find their worth in whatever people are willing to pay. Gold and silver, in particular, feel more secure when the economy becomes volatile. Those who put precious metals in their safe strive to hedge against inflation and protect against the growing national debt.

With the growing debt in this country, some gold and silver owners have invested in this store of value to buy time and protect their wealth for the future. The chart below demonstrates the attraction. As the national debt increases, the price of gold rises as well. When fear sets in because of inflation, a rocky political atmosphere, or the economy, the price will typically go higher. When everything seems peaceful, the price generally goes down.

	VAL	ANN
● US Public Debt (I:USPD)	34.00T	8.40%
Gold Price in US Dollars (I:GPUSD)	2214.40	5.17%

Sep 5, 2024, 11:56 AM EDT Powered by YCHARTS

The History of the Dollar

Many prefer gold and silver as a store of value over cash because of the truth of the value of money. When we hold dollar bills in our hands, we really hold instruments that represent the debt of the United States government. Up until the seventies, every dollar was backed by gold or silver; you could exchange it for precious metal. Some currency had the words "Silver Certificate" printed under the picture of the president because it represented the silver the government held.

The demise of the gold standard began during World War I when countries around the globe printed more currency than they had gold to back it to meet the demands created by the conflict. By 1973, even the United States decided to abandon this age-old way of backing money. Around the world, fiat money became the standard. This simply means each government puts value on the bills in circulation and gives them legal tender status.

> The paper money in and of itself has no real value other than the full faith and credit of the United States government.

The paper money in and of itself has no real value other than the full faith and credit of the United States government. This is why the wealthy typically have gold and silver as a portion of their investment portfolio.

Cryptocurrency

Though I'm not a fan of cryptocurrency as an investment strategy, I'd be remiss if I didn't mention this area. Bitcoin, Ethereum, and other cryptocurrencies have been rising in popularity for years. Like precious metals, they offer no cash flow, and their value is determined by what people are willing to pay along with many other outside, hard-to-predict, volatile influences (this is why I listed them in the "other commodities" camp). Additionally, when you begin to purchase cryptocurrency, you have to figure in the chance of security breaches and technology failure.

If you decide to invest in crypto, it's vital you understand exactly what you are getting into. Study the field and get advice from an experienced advisor. To protect your investment from hackers, it's a good idea to store your Bitcoin or other cryptocurrency in your digital wallet.

While I know a few wealthy who have stepped into the world of crypto, they don't trade in it. Most stay with gold and silver if they decide to go the commodity route. Typically, people prefer what they understand. Crypto reminds me of a flying car. We know the technology exists, and it may be a reality in the future; however, we feel safer with what we can touch and see. Everyone understands their Starbucks latte or a '57 Chevy. We know what to do with them and feel comfortable there. The vast number of unknowns and variables make crypto a less secure and undesirable place for me to store my money.

Now that you're familiar with all five super asset classes, it's time to move into the Super Power Plays[IP] you can harness by combining strategies.

CHAPTER NINE
SUPERCHARGE YOUR POWER PLAYS

Now that you have the basics of the five super asset classes and how they can create wealth, cash flow, as well as save you money on your taxes, it's time to combine strategies to supercharge our Power Plays. The more areas we can take advantage of, the more it begins to look like the opposing team had to put two, three, or four players in the penalty box.

When you start to move business income into oil and gas or real estate, instead of writing a check to the IRS, you may find them sending one to you. Between the depreciation, expenses, depletion deductions, and more, you can use your cash flow to purchase other producing assets and maximize your refund.

In every asset class except commodities, you can create strategies to see cash flow. But the wealthy don't hoard it and allow the government to take 40 percent, they use the Power Plays we've already talked about and more. Below, I'm going to give you some scenarios that I call Super Power Plays, but don't limit yourself to these. When you begin to combine strategies, the possibilities are almost endless!

Super Power Plays

Super Power Play 1: If you've turned your business into a corporation or an LLC, you can currently deduct up to 20 percent of your qualified business income (QBI). However, after your taxable income reaches a certain threshold, the IRS begins to decrease the amount of QBI you can deduct. To reduce your tax, you can invest in an oil and gas drilling program with intangible losses and lower your taxable income, so you can get back some of your QBI deduction.

Super Power Play 2: Those who start a business soon begin to see the advantages that the deductions associated with entrepreneurship can bring. But even better, after your business starts to grow and cash flow increases, you can leverage a Super Power Play to minimize your taxes and maximize your income. By investing in real estate with your excess business income, you can enjoy your business deductions, as well as the various real estate Power Plays.

Chapter 9

Own a Business and Buy Real Estate

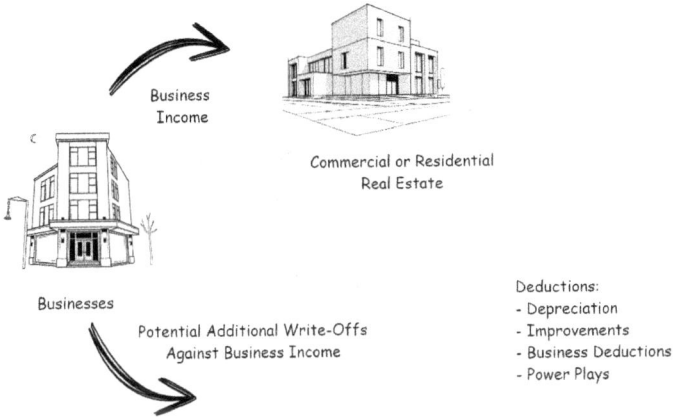

Business
Income

Commercial or Residential
Real Estate

Businesses

Potential Additional Write-Offs
Against Business Income

Deductions:
- Depreciation
- Improvements
- Business Deductions
- Power Plays

For example, let's say you have $150,000 in passive deductions on your real estate, but you realized only $100,000 in passive income. First, you can use deductions to offset all your passive real estate income. Next, if you or your spouse are a real estate professional, you can write the additional $50,000 in passive expenses off of your active business income. This could reduce your tax liability by an additional $20,000 if you are in the 40 percent tax bracket.

Super Power Play 3: Some traditional qualified retirement plans, for example, 401(k)s and traditional IRAs, have *required minimum distributions* (RMD). If you're forced to take an RMD that is much larger than you need or want, especially if it moves you into a high tax bracket, you can redirect these funds into oil and gas and take the write-off.

Let's assume your required distribution is $300,000 and you have income from other sources. You could take $100,000 and invest in an oil and gas drilling program. Because you potentially can write off nearly 90 percent of your income in the year you invest in production, instead of paying $40,000 in taxes on that $100,000–assuming a 40 percent tax bracket, you may only pay $4,000. And you can return the $36,000 saving to your paper assets to grow your cash flow, while enjoying the full $100,000 investment in oil and gas.

Chapter 9

Large IRA Distributions to Oil & Gas

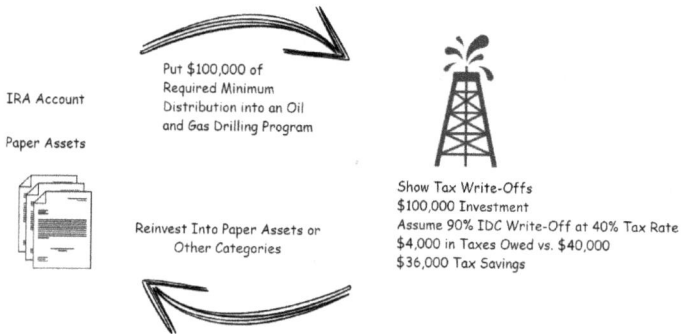

IRA Account

Paper Assets

Put $100,000 of Required Minimum Distribution into an Oil and Gas Drilling Program

Reinvest Into Paper Assets or Other Categories

Show Tax Write-Offs
$100,000 Investment
Assume 90% IDC Write-Off at 40% Tax Rate
$4,000 in Taxes Owed vs. $40,000
$36,000 Tax Savings

Super Power Play 4: Does your employer have a profit-sharing plan that offers company stock? If so, you'll want to look at the *net unrealized appreciation* (NUA) Strategy. In a qualified retirement plan, company stock gets special tax treatment if it's addressed properly. Historically, Procter & Gamble, headquartered in Cincinnati, has contributed company stock with a very low cost basis into a profit-sharing plan. Imagine a scenario where the stock is trading at $160 a share, but the cost basis is only $6.80 a share. Using the NUA strategy, at regular retirement or another properly defined time, the employee may take his or her shares out of the qualified plan and move them into a brokerage account. The retiree will pay standard income tax on the cost basis only, while the remainder gain will be treated as a long-term capital gain. This benefit from the IRS tax code and your company can be an excellent way to combine tax environments to minimize taxes on cash flow. There are rules around this and you may wish to consult a fee-only advisor to assist.

Super Power Play 5: Take the funds you receive from oil and gas production and invest in commodities like precious metals to hedge against inflation.

Alternatively, you could dump them back into oil and gas. If you took $80,000 from your oil and gas cash flow and reinvested it in drilling, you could save close to $29,000 in taxes if you were in the 40 percent bracket.

Chapter 9

Oil & Gas To Other Commodities

Cash Flow
$80,000   or   Back To Oil & Gas

(Additional Tax Savings of
approximately $29,000 at
a 40% Tax Rate)

Gold & Silver

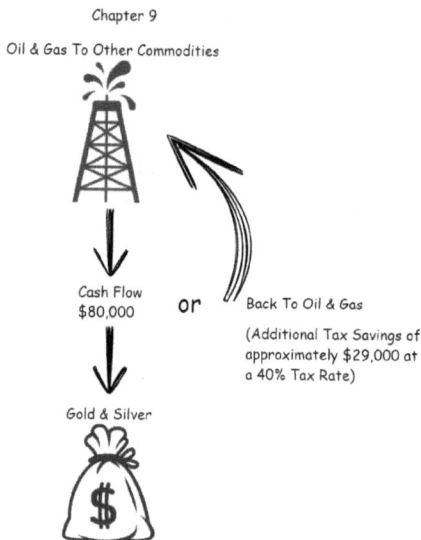

Super Power Play 6: OK, here is a Super Power Play you can implement anytime. Our goal is to always focus on being a producer first and a consumer second, even when we look to "consume."

Let's assume you have been working hard and saved enough to purchase a new $100,000 luxury automobile. You have to choose between paying with cash or financing and making monthly payments. Most who have the money would plan on paying with cash. But what would happen if we changed our thinking?

Instead of figuring out how to purchase something to consume, we want to find a way to buy an asset that will provide enough cash flow to make the monthly payments. For example, you could purchase a piece of real estate, use the $100,00 as a downpayment, and finance the car. In this scenario, the income will make the car payments; however, at the end of the payment plan, you will not only own a car outright, you will also own an asset that will continue to provide cash flow and write-offs through depreciation. Better yet, take as many write-offs on the car as you can by using it in your business.

I encourage you to play this "game": Do not allow yourself to outright buy the larger items you want to purchase. Instead, make a decision to buy an asset and use the cash flow from the asset to purchase the item.

The Ultimate Power Plays

Few have time to carry out the Ultimate Power Plays on their own. The scenarios are exponential. As cash flow increases, you can move your new income into other asset classes. Plus, if you invest even one-half of your tax savings into these revenue streams, your potential to vacation more often, live a little more extravagantly in your retirement, or be more philanthropic increase.

Let's see how combining all of the super asset classes can bring your wealth and cash flow up, while driving taxes down.

Chapter 9
One Ultimate Super Power Play

Businesses

Business Income
$500,000

Commercial or Residential
Investment Property
$2,000,000 Building

Passive $80,000 Income
No Income Taxes Because of Deductions

Paper Assets

Tax Deductions

Deductibles & Write-Offs

More Real Estate

Income From Real Estate
(Assume $80,000)

$80,000 at 40% Income Tax Rate and 90% IDCs
Government is now paying you
$29,000 back because $80,000
Tax-Free from Real Estate &
Now Additional Write-Offs on same $80,000

Private Equity

$40,000 Income 1st Year
(Only $34,000 Taxable)

More Oil & Gas
Additional Incentives

Other Commodities
(Gold/Silver)

Let's assume Brit owns a business and has fully funded her retirement plans to maximize her tax deductions in the paper asset world. To maximize her strategy, Brit decides to invest $500,000 of her business income into the other super asset classes.

Assuming her business income falls in the 40 percent tax rate, she could expect a $200,000 tax bill on her half million. She can save on taxes and build her assets by taking this $500,000 and using it to make a down payment on a $2,000,000 piece of residential real estate. After she pays her mortgage, her passive annual income will be $80,000. However, the deductions she can take in year one add up to $137,000, making this tax-free revenue income (Remember from the Real Estate chapter we are assuming a full year of deductibility in year one). Since her husband is a real estate professional, they can take the additional $57,000 and write it off against business income—an additional tax savings of $22,800.

Because Brit is trying to be a producer first, she takes the $80,000 from her real estate endeavor and invests in an oil and gas drilling program towards year end. Assuming a 90 percent write-off, she will get back an additional $29,000 of tax savings for the $80,000 investment made. Did you catch that?! The $80,000 income from real estate that is not being taxed, is now being used to generate additional tax savings of $29,000! Calculate that infinite return.

Now, let's assume that the income from the oil and gas production is $40,000 the first year. The depletion allowance means only $34,000 of this will be taxable. Her strategy opens the door for her to do any number of things with this additional $40,000 in cash flow from oil and gas:

1. Purchase $40,000 of commodities for protection.

2. Add to paper assets in publicly traded investments or private equity.

3. Add this to additional assets to purchase more real estate.

4. Add this back into more oil and gas.

If Brit had opted not to purchase the real estate, her $500,000 income would have been taxed at 40 percent, leaving her with $300,000 to invest.

Using this Ultimate Power Play, she now owns real estate valued at $2,000,000 with $80,000 in tax-free income each year and a tax reduction on her business income of $22,800. She also has an oil and gas investment of $80,000 that gives her an additional $29,000 in tax savings. Plus, Brit opted to use her $40,000 savings to invest in gold and silver.

So, let's add this up:

	Income	Taxes
Business:	$500,000	$200,000
Real Estate:	$80,000	-$22,800
Oil and Gas:	$40,000	-$29,000

So, prior to the purchase of her commodities, she increased her cash flow to $620,000 from $500,000, reduced her taxes by almost $52,000, and owns a $2,000,000 piece of real estate and $80,000 in oil and gas that will keep producing cash flow. Can you see the power in this?

If she had purchased commercial real estate instead of residential and taken advantage of the current tax laws, she could have had $448,000 of first year deductions and wiped out an additional $124,000 in taxes after the rental income because of the real estate professional activity, bringing the total tax to just $28,000 and reducing her effective tax rate to roughly 4.5 percent instead of 40 percent on the $620,000 of income (Remember from the Real Estate chapter, we are only assuming Bonus Depreciation is being used in year one for improvements and contents).

	Income	Taxes
Business:	$500,000	$200,000
Real Estate:	$80,000	-$142,800
Oil and Gas:	$40,000	-$29,000

After she purchased the silver and gold, because of no additional deductions, she'll owe an additional tax of $13,600, 40 percent of the $34,000 from the oil and gas income the following year.

Now you see the potential power of combining the Power Plays into Ultimate Power Plays. I have provided one structure in my example, however there are many combinations that could be built. What mix will you choose when you build your Ultimate Power Play?

PART THREE

PREVAIL

CHAPTER TEN
MAXIMIZE YOUR POTENTIAL

I could have easily written a whole book on each chapter. But my goal was to give you an introduction to the strategies the wealthy use. And one of those strategies that I've repeated throughout the book might be the most important takeaway. Finding a fee-only wealth advisor and a great tax firm will probably be the most valuable asset for your financial growth.

Your second most important strategy will be to keep learning and looking for ways to take action. Every new small step counts. Fee-only advisors can help create asset allocation strategies that focus on your level of risk and return for which you are seeking. They do more than

Keep learning and looking for ways to take action.

merely invest your money for you. A good wealth advisor helps you rebalance your accounts, recognizes your behavioral tendencies, provides coaching and asset location, and advises on the most prudent spending and reinvestment strategies. When your emotions try to drive you to buy and sell assets, a wealth advisor can help you see the most rational route by removing the emotions of fear and greed. Our goal is to prevent clients from doing the wrong things at the wrong time.

Vanguard did a study that revealed most investors believed they were 16 percent closer to their financial goals because they had a human advisor. Those who had digital advisors felt only about 5 percent closer to their financial goals.[10] Another Vanguard study showed an advisor may increase the value of your portfolio by up to 3 percent a year.[11] You are an expert in your field, it's important to find an expert in the financial world to assist you in maximizing your cash flow and minimizing the amount you pay during tax season.

I've only touched the tip of the iceberg in each chapter of this book. As I said at the beginning, "Knowledge is power." I encourage you to dig deeper to find solutions that best suit your financial situation. Fortunately, there's a vast array of information to be found. To make it easy for you, I've compiled some of my best advice in my blog and in videos that accompany the topics in this book. I'll be the first to admit, I don't have a corner on the knowledge you'll find at this QR code; however, to save you from searching the entire internet, I've expanded on the subjects and gathered them all in one place.

It's Time to Put the Power Plays to Work for You

I want everyone to discover ways to harness the Power Plays I've mentioned in this book. Even if you have to start small, with a bit of determination and some mentoring, anyone can play this game.

I'm certain something in these pages resonated with you. That's the best place to start! You've probably heard it said, "Don't leave money on the table." I offer the same advice when it comes to increasing your cash flow and leveraging the tax laws. If the wealthiest in our country avoid the highest tax brackets, why shouldn't you? Move to action. Leverage the Power Plays of the Wealthy starting today.

APPENDIX

QUESTIONS TO ASK A RETIREMENT PLAN PROVIDER

- Do I have to elect contributions for bonuses and my regular pay or is it all one selection?
- What is the vesting schedule?
- How much is the participant currently contributing? (percentage or dollar amount)
- What is the company match?
- Are there limitations on what percentage of my pay may I contribute to my 401(k)?
- IF YOU ARE ELIGIBLE FOR BONUSES: Does the same limit apply to my bonus earnings as well as my regular income?
- Am I allowed to contribute after-tax funds into the plan?

- Is a Roth 401(k) source available within the plan?

- If I make an after-tax contribution into my account, may I convert that to the Roth 401(k) source?

- If I make an after-tax contribution into my account, may I do a rollover conversion into a Roth IRA outside of my plan?

- Can participants roll money from a pretax source into a Roth IRA directly at their firm automatically or is a phone call required?

- Will my contributions be suspended in any way if I roll the pretax funds into a Roth IRA as a conversion outside of the plan?

- Am I allowed to do unlimited conversions from the after-tax source into the Roth source or Roth IRA conversion /rollover? If so, how many conversions/rollovers may I do per year/quarter?

- If I am either doing an in-plan conversion or a rollover Roth IRA conversion, will the plan allow me to convert automatically, or do I have to call in to do this each time?

- Does the company offer a true up match if I max out my contribution too early?

IF RELEVANT:

- Is the participant allowed to do rollovers at age fifty-nine and a half if still employed?

- Is there a Guaranteed Investment Contract (GIC)?

- Is a Brokerage Link or Personal Choice Retirement Account (PCRA) option available?

ENDNOTES

1 *Iris.* "How Many Pages Is the Tax Code?" Updated June 23, 2022. https://irisreading.com/how-long-would-it-take-to-read-the-entire-u-s-tax-code/.

2 *St. Jude Children's Research Hospital.* "Facts for Media." Accessed October 3, 2024. https://www.stjude.org/media-resources/media-tools/facts.htm.

3 Grant, Alexis. *AlexisGrant.com.* "Businesses that Begin as Side Hustles are More Likely to Succeed." September 22, 2104. https://alexisgrant.com/2014/09/22/why-side-hustle-new-study/.

4 Kinsey, Doug. *Investopedia.* "Advisor Insight in Which Has Performed Better Historically Stock Market or Real Estate." June 22, 2024. https://www.investopedia.com/ask/answers/052015/which-has-performed-better-historically-stock-market-or-real-estate.asp.

5   Davis, G. Brian. *BiggerPockets*. "Real Estate
    vs. Stocks: What 145 Years of Returns
    Tell Us." Updated March 10, 2023.
    https://www.biggerpockets.com/blog/
    real-estate-vs-stocks-performance.

6   Jayanti, Suriya. "Think the Energy Crisis
    Is Bad? Wait Until Next Winter." *Time.*
    October 31, 2022. https://time.com/6226587/
    energy-crisis-next-winter/.

7   Ibid.

8   *U.S. Energy Development Corporation Oil and Gas
    Tax Handbook for Opportunity Zones*, 2023.

9   Hwang, Inyoung. "A Brief History of the Stock
    Market and Stock Exchanges." *Sofi.* February
    27, 2024. https://www.sofi.com/learn/content/
    history-of-the-stock-market/.

10 *Vanguard.* "Valuing Advice." Accessed October
    18, 2024. https://advisors.vanguard.com/
    advisors-alpha/advice-that-clients-value.

11 Kinniry, Jr., Francis M., Colleen M. Jaconetti,
    Michael A. DiJoseph, David J. Walker, and
    Maria C. Quinn. "Putting a value on your
    value: Quantifying Vanguard Advisor's Alpha."
    Vanguard Investment Advisory Research Center.
    July 2022. https://advisors.vanguard.com/
    insights/article/putting-a-value-on-your-value-
    quantifying-advisors-alpha

ACKNOWLEDGMENTS

To my daughters: Rachel, Aleigha, Marisa, Miriam, and Rivers. Thank you for life more abundant. I look forward to more adventures together.

To my sons-in-law: Thomas and Philip. Thank you for joining this crazy life journey with us.

To my Team Members at Harvest Financial Advisors: Thank you for always bringing excellence to our clients and respect to each other. You are an inspiration to me. I look forward to our next 10X growth together.

ABOUT THE AUTHOR

Marc Henn is the Chief Executive Officer and Founder of Harvest Financial Advisors, LLC, which is head-quartered in Cincinnati, OH. In his role, he helps business owners, executives, retirees, and entrepreneurs transform their financial lives to find abundance, purpose, and peace of mind. He has been featured or quoted in many publications including *Barron's*, *The Wall Street Journal*, and *Financial Planning Magazine*.

Recognizing the transformative power of education, he regularly speaks with various groups of all ages on many financial topics, especially investing and taxes, and how understanding the intersection of these two areas is vital for those who want to create wealth. He also has a passion for paying forward what he has learned, through teaching and planning for the next generation.

Marc is a Certified Financial Planner® Professional (CFP®) and has been assisting family office and wealth management clients for thirty-five years. He is a 1990 graduate of Purdue University, earning a Bachelor of Science in Economics. Marc enjoys organic gardening, reading, and telling a good dad joke. He lives in Cincinnati with his wife and loves creating adventures with his family.